SACRED BETRAYALS

Martha Alegría Reichmann de Valladares

SACRED BETRAYALS

A widow raises her voice
against the corruption of
the Francis papacy

Foreword by Archbishop
Carlo Maria Viganò

Translated, edited, and adapted
in close cooperation
with the author
by Matthew Cullinan Hoffman

FAITHFUL INSIGHT BOOKS

FRONT ROYAL, VIRGINIA

Traiciones Sagradas (Spanish original)
© 2019 Martha Alegría Reichmann.
ilisom@yahoo.com

Sacred Betrayals (English translation and adaptation of *Traiciones Sagradas*, as well as additional introductory material and annotations)
© 2021 Faithful Insight Books / LifeSiteNews.com

ISBN 978-1-7352671-0-4
Library of Congress Control Number: 2020949191

Faithful Insight Books
4 Family Life Lane
Front Royal, VA 22630
USA
www.faithfulinsight.com

Articles originally published in Italian and Spanish by *L'Espresso*, Confidencial Honduras, and Criterio.hn appearing in this book have been translated and reprinted with permission from the copyright owners, for which the author and publisher express their gratitude.

Cover foreground taken from a personal photo of Martha Alegría Reichmann de Valladares with Martha (left), her husband Alejandro Valladares Lanza (right), and Cardinal Óscar Andrés Rodríguez Maradiaga (center), superimposed over image of dome of St. Peter's Basilica, and placed within an image of a frame. Cover designed by Jason Taylor.

This book, which is a formal denunciation before the world, I wish to dedicate to all of the priests and laity who have been persecuted by Cardinal Óscar Andrés Rodríguez Maradiaga for the sole reason of having informed him about the misconduct of his auxiliary bishop Juan José Pineda Fasquelle, some of whom are named in this book, while others remain in anonymity. I want to say to them that their voices of clamor are in mine and that here the word of God is being fulfilled: "That which you have spoken in the ear in the chambers, shall be preached on the housetops" (Luke 12:3).

CONTENTS

ACKNOWLEDGEMENTS AND CLARIFICATIONS

Martha Alegría Reichmann de Valladares

I am infinitely grateful to Almighty God for clearly showing me the path to take for writing and publishing this story, for giving me clear ideas and placing the right people at the right time to help me carry it to a successful completion, so that it may be read by thousands of people who are aware that there is only one way: Jesus Christ.

A very special thank you

When I published my book in Spanish, I had the desire to publish it also in English, but soon I realized that doing it on my own was practically impossible; at that moment and somewhat discouraged, I took a copy of my book in Spanish, wrapped it in the canvas I keep with the image of the Face of Jesus and said to him: "Dear Jesus, I have done everything I could do, if you want more, do it, because I can no longer continue. I leave everything in your hands. The decision is yours, Lord." I placed it on a piece of furniture in front of a picture of the face of Jesus resurrected and exactly five days later I received a letter from a LifeSite reporter in which he told me that my book had reached his hands and when he read it he was quite impressed, and he asked me if I was ready for them to publish an English edition because they considered it very important. His name is Matthew Cullinan Hoffman. I responded immediately without thinking twice, accepting his proposal and explaining to him that I believed he was an instrument of God because the response I had received was immediate, surprising, mind-blowing, and wonderful.

God put my book not in the hands of a publisher but in the hands of one of the most prestigious media in the Catholic world with over 100 million page views a year, but which had been unknown to me up to that time. I believe they were chosen by God to help the truth prevail in a world of lies and hypocrisy.

Thank you, Matthew. Thank you John-Henry Westen and Steve Jalsevac, co-founders of LifeSite, for carrying out this project, which, more than mine and yours, is a project of God.

From the bottom of my heart I also thank all the people who have given me their moral support in one way or another, and who have addressed beautiful words and phrases to me, showing me solidarity, appreciation and understanding. I wish also to thank the prelates who have attended to me in the course of this story, as well as the people who have seen my interviews without having met me personally and have approached me simply to give me a word of support or to offer me help, ranging from humble folk to important professionals, such as the lawyer James Bogle who searched for me from London. I also wish to thank the Italian Cavalliere Silvano Pedrollo. I warmly thank all those people who have courageously published serious and conscientious articles commenting on the abominable abuses of Cardinal Rodríguez Maradiaga and who in their writings have not failed to mention my case, such as Mr. Marlon Avila Amador, engineer Maria Guadalupe Cisneros Vaquedano, Mr. José Matías Vásquez Enamorado and Virginia Marisol Aguirre of the Parish of Our Lady of Fatima of Siguatepeque, Father Bernardo Font Ribot, Mr. Carlos Humberto Oseguera, and the ex-nuncio to the United States, Archbishop Carlo Maria Viganò. I would also like to thank the prestigious Vaticanists Marco Tosatti and Aldo Maria Valli, and all of the bloggers who have written about my case.

I wish to thank the international media that have opened their doors to me, especially the prestigious journalists Emiliano Fittipaldi, Gabriel Ariza Rossi and Edward Pentin for their interest in interviewing me and publishing my articles, making it clear to me that my case has touched hearts. I am also grateful to the few media in my country that dare with nobility and courage, to denounce what others do not dare, thus gaining more and more prestige both nationally and internationally: Confidential Honduras, Criterio.hn, Une TV, Reporteros de Investigación, and the eminent newspaper *El Libertador*. I would also like to thank the reporter Valentina Alazraki, who interviewed me for Televisa. I also want to thank Archbishop Carlo Maria Viganò, Philip Lawler, and Henry Sire for lending their public words of support to the publication of this work. My thanks to everyone who has written words of support through social networks and directly to my email. I ask that God bless them always.

Clarification

Like other authors, I would also like to clarify that I am writing this book with the authority conferred on me by canon 212, article 3, of the Code of Canon Law, which states the following: "According to the knowledge, competence, and prestige which they possess, they have the right and even at times the duty to manifest to the sacred pastors their opinion on matters which pertain to the good of the Church and to make their opinion known to the rest of the Christian faithful, without prejudice to the integrity of faith and morals, with reverence toward their pastors, and attentive to common advantage and the dignity of persons." I regard it as my duty to report the facts that I relate in this book.

Moreover, I am fully convinced that I am acting according to the commands of our Lord Jesus Christ that are given to me in the Holy Scriptures, and if anyone feels offended or upset, the only thing he has to do is to examine his conscience exhaustively, rather than seeking guilt in other people.

Let it be known that I am prepared for everything from fire-crackers to missiles because I have put on the "armor of God." If you attack me, don't do it with lies and slander because I know how to defend myself. I am strong in the LORD. In the custody of my lawyer there is more evidence that I cannot publish because of its confidentiality, but it is there. In any case, all I am doing is telling a story as it truly happened and reinforcing it with evidence.

I also want to clarify that I began to write this story not with the intention of publishing it, but with the intention of releasing my tensions, of shaking off the indignation for feeling trampled, humiliated and betrayed. I needed to write and write to get rid of possible psychological damage and to avoid falling into a deep depression. But God showed me the way, and later you will read about the spark that brought me to finally decide to bring this story to light. I'm sorry to do this without the support of my two daughters who are fearful of the risks I am running, but I cannot deny the voice of God, who is requesting it of me.

The substance of this book may be reduced to this: I AM LOYAL TO GOD, NOT TO MAN. I am not loyal to those who sink the Church. I am not loyal to false prophets. A cardinal committed an injustice against me, and that helped to open my eyes and I began gradually learning of other evils. This matter is so serious and so grave it cannot remain in the darkness. What I relate here is very little; what remains unreported is vast.

I have entrusted this work to Saint Michael the Archangel as my protector. I have also asked him to reveal the truth about those prelates who have raised their cassocks to give room to the devil, where he is at ease, enjoying himself and doing much harm.

FOREWORD

Archbishop Carlo Maria Viganò

Former Secretary-General of the Governorate of Vatican City State and Apostolic Nuncio to the United States

When I gave my first public testimony in August of 2018 regarding corruption and sexual abuse cover-ups in the Holy See, a great media storm arose focusing on the case of Cardinal Theodore McCarrick, whose record of sexual abuse had been known by Pope Bergoglio since at least 2013, when I personally informed him of it. Only almost six year later, Francis laicized McCarrick in an act that served to reinforce his image as a reformer and simultaneously to draw attention away from numerous other accusations of corruption. In so doing, Francis had been covering up the horrible crimes of McCarrick for almost six years, exposing other potential victims to his horrifying abuses.

As I pointed out to the Washington Post in June of 2019, the international media became so distracted with the McCarrick case that they ultimately failed to follow up with investigations into these accusations, which often touch upon the person of the pope himself. In that interview, I gave as a prime example the case of Cardinal Óscar Andrés Rodríguez Maradiaga, Archbishop of Tegucigalpa, Honduras, known as the "vice pope," who has been accused repeatedly of grave acts of malfeasance and cover-ups in his diocese.

Cardinal Maradiaga is widely seen as the most powerful of all the cardinals due to his closeness to and influence on the pope.

Together with Cardinal McCarrick, he has acted as a "kingmaker" in deciding appointments in the Vatican curia as well as for important sees internationally. As coordinator of the Council of Cardinal Advisers, he was and is organizing a major reform of the structure of the Vatican curia itself. A string of articles in the Italian, American, and Honduran media had all along these years exposed a massive scandal of both financial corruption and a web of homosexual misconduct connected to Maradiaga and his auxiliary bishop, Juan José Pineda. Maradiaga is also alleged to have advocated for the very important appointment of Substitute of the Secretariat of State Archbishop Edgar Peña Parra, accused of having sexually abused a minor seminarian and of persistent immoral behavior.

After an extensive Vatican investigation with interviews of dozens of witnesses to the corruption, Francis had done nothing and even defended Maradiaga publicly. The pope did not retreat from his defense of the cardinal even after an explosion of accusations of sexual abuse in the Tegucigalpa seminary. After months of negative media coverage, he finally allowed Pineda to resign from his position, but without any punishment.

I had already commented on the Maradiaga scandal in my original testimony, noting that Maradiaga "is so confident of the Pope's protection that he can dismiss as 'gossip' the heartfelt appeals of dozens of his seminarians, who found the courage to write to him after one of them tried to commit suicide over homosexual abuse in the seminary. By now the faithful have well understood Maradiaga's strategy: insult the victims to save himself, lie to the bitter end to cover up a chasm of abuses of power, of mismanagement in the administration of Church property, and of financial disasters even against close friends, as in the case of the Ambassador of Honduras Alejandro Valladares, former Dean of the Diplomatic Corps to the Holy See."

I also noted that the very troubling accusations against Bishop Pineda had been swept under the rug following his resignation, and called on Pope Francis to release the results of the

Holy See's investigation: "Regarding Pineda the only thing that has been made public is that his resignation has simply been accepted, thus making any possible responsibility of his and Maradiaga vanish into nowhere. In the name of the transparency so hailed by the Pope, the report that the Visitator, Argentine bishop Alcides Casaretto, delivered more than a year ago only and directly to the Pope, must be made public." However, this has never been done.

Moreover, as I alluded to in my original testimony, the widow of the former ambassador to the Holy See for Honduras, who had been a close personal friend of Cardinal Maradiaga, Martha Alegría Reichmann, had recently testified to her own knowledge of the cardinal's corrupt conduct in an important new book in Spanish, "Traiciones Sagradas" ("Sacred Betrayals"). Yet the international media had failed to take notice and to follow up on this, to follow the leads the book provides and to question Cardinal Maradiaga and Bergoglio about the matter. I again called for such an investigation in my Washington Post interview in 2019:

"Journalists should be digging for the facts, interviewing the victims, following the money and promotion trails, and uncovering the corrupt networks. There are so many cases to go after. Just to cite one: Have you read the recent book by Martha Alegria Reichmann, about the misdeeds of Cardinal Maradiaga, chosen by Pope Francis as a trusted senior adviser, in fact the head of the C-9 council? Have you thought of interviewing her? Of investigating her claims? Of requesting an interview with Maradiaga to ask him about all the accusations that have been leveled against him? Of asking Pope Francis why he picked such a man as his adviser?"

Martha Alegría's book was published in Honduras by a small publishing house and was not very accessible to the international media. However, I am very pleased that her book has now been translated and adapted to English by Faithful Insight Books, the publishing imprint of LifeSite, an important news service in the coverage of corruption in the Catholic Church.

I deeply regret that the *Washington Post*, usually very professional in denouncing corruption in society, failed to pursue an investigation on this matter I raised in my above-mentioned interview. The English translation of Martha Alegría's book offers the *Post* a new opportunity to do so by making known her book, which reveals her great concern for the existence of a deep-rooted corruption in the Church in Honduras that involves the Pope himself.

Alegría's husband was a close friend of Archbishop Maradiaga and played a crucial role in his career, using his position as ambassador to the Holy See to lobby successfully for his elevation to the rank of cardinal. As Delegate for the Papal Representations, I personally knew Ambassador Valladares, and met with him on several occasions. In his duties as Dean of the Diplomatic Corps, he had the privilege of addressing the Holy Father and the superiors of the Secretariat of State in official ceremonies, on behalf of the Diplomatic Corps. I always appreciated his great competence and skills, as well as his insightfulness, clarity of thought and amiability of character.

Alegría's testimony regarding Cardinal Maradiaga's involvement of their family in a fraudulent financial scheme, as well as his defense and cover-ups of his auxiliary bishop is deeply shocking. More disturbing is her revelation that Francis continues to protect Maradiaga despite all the misdeeds for which Maradiaga has made himself personally responsible. Her personal perspective also enables us to see the sinister complicity of Francis with Maradiaga, who lobbied for the pope's election. Under Pope Francis, Maradiaga appears to be "untouchable," no matter how vile and horrendous his offenses may be. The same is true of many other officials of the Francis papacy.

I hope that with the release of this important personal testimony by such an eminent witness, the widow of the dean of the Vatican's diplomatic corps, the international media and the Catholic faithful in general will turn its attention to this grave scandal and insist on receiving answers from Pope Bergoglio and the Vatican curia. This terrible crisis of sexual abuse, financial corruption, and naked impunity in the Church will end only when our prelates begin to practice what they preach, and are held accountable publicly for their malfeasance. By the grace of God, and the insistence of the faithful, may it be done!

INTRODUCTION

Matthew Cullinan Hoffman

For almost forty years, Martha Alegría Reichmann and her husband, Ambassador Alejandro Valladares, were among the closest friends of Óscar Andrés Rodríguez Maradiaga, the influential archbishop and cardinal who became the coordinator of Pope Francis' Council of Cardinal Advisers, and who has been dubbed by the Italian media as the "vice pope." The Valladares's home was his habitual residence in Rome, the place where he stayed and ate the meals they prepared for him, and where he often celebrated Christmas with a family that he claimed to love as if they were his own. His friend and later auxiliary bishop, Juan José Pineda Fasquelle, also became a close friend and frequent guest of the family for decades. The Valladareses believed they knew the duo well, and were grateful for their friendship, which had been one of mutual trust and support, a constant anchor in their lives.

In the space of a few short years their illusions about the two would be shattered completely. The family's life savings would be lost in a fraudulent investment scheme promoted to them by the cardinal, who had suddenly begun to act as if he did not know them. Pineda Fasquelle would refuse to return precious historical documents that they had lent to him, and would begin a whispering campaign to end Valladares's ambassadorship. As Martha Alegría, finally widowed and desperate, searched for answers and sought justice from the Holy See, reporters would uncover evidence that Maradiaga himself had invested and supposedly lost, in the same financial scam, over a million dollars in funds that had been donated to the diocese. Moreover, each year the cardinal was removing close to half a million dollars from the University of Honduras for unaccounted-for expenditures, and an additional 1.3 million dollars of government grant money given to the Church had disappeared in the hands of Bishop Pineda, equally unaccounted for.

The money trail led not only to a fraudulent investment scheme that had disappeared without a trace, but also to several close male favorites of Bishop Pineda, who was accused of lavishing cars and other benefits on them, sharing his rooms with them on trips, and even bringing them to live with him in the residence of the archbishop, Villa Iris. Pineda's disturbing lifestyle, which also reportedly included first class air trips to visit male friends in Spain, automobile and real estate purchases, and other luxuries, was ruthlessly covered up by Cardinal Maradiaga, who penalized anyone who protested against the abuses of his protégé. Accusations of homosexual predation by Pineda against seminarians had also arisen and were being reported to the apostolic nuncio in Honduras. The reports were a troubling confirmation of much of what Alegría Reichmann had heard in her own informal conversations with clergy and other close associates of the cardinal and his auxiliary.

However, Alegría Reichmann was in for an even greater shock. After she and approximately fifty others complained to the apostolic nuncio in Honduras and an official Vatican investigation was launched, and after she brought her complaint directly to Pope Francis himself in a private audience, she found that the pontiff's promised help never materialized. Instead the pope would stand behind his ally, a man who had helped to elect him to the papacy and was now the head of his highly influential Vatican reform committee. The well-connected cardinal enjoyed the most powerful protection of all: that of the supreme pontiff himself. The Valladares family, and all the others who had been victimized by Maradiaga's corrupt regime, would receive no justice from Pope Francis.

To understand the significance of this story, its place in the context of the Francis pontificate must first be examined.

An unprecedented papacy

The Catholic Church today is faced with the sad spectacle of what is arguably the most troubled and confused papacy in its bimillennial history, a reality that is shaking the institution to its foundations and sowing scandal and confusion among both clergy and laity.

It can be said in this unfortunate sense that the pontificate of Pope Francis is *sui generis* in the long annals of the See of Rome. Unlike previous cases of ecclesiastical corruption, in which scandals were confined to the personal immorality of the pontiff or his appointees or to mere weakness and confusion in defending orthodox Catholic doctrine, the Francis papacy has shown signs of a systemic corruption at every level: personal, financial, and doctrinal.

The subversive acts against Catholic doctrine by the regime of Francis are now too many to be adequately enumerated in the space of a brief essay. The pope is perhaps most infamous for his statements in the encyclical *Amoris laetitia* that seem to affirm that adultery and other intrinsically evil acts can be justified if they are undertaken to avoid some other, presumably worse, evil,[1] and that those who are publicly living in adulterous second marriages should be able to undertake leadership and liturgical roles in the Church and even to receive Holy Communion.[2] Bishops and theologians are now using the same reasoning to legitimize homosexual relationships, and have

---

[1] *Amoris laetitia* 301.
[2] *Amoris laetitia* 305; "Epistula Apostolica ad Excellentissimum Dominum Sergium Alfredum Fenoy," *Acta Apostolicae Sedis* (October) 2016, p. 1071-1074.

received no correction for such statements.[3] The pontiff has also stated publicly that contraception, which was condemned as intrinsically evil by Pope Paul VI and Pope John Paul II, can be justified in difficult cases,[4] and has condemned the death penalty, the legitimacy of which has always been affirmed by the Catholic Church, as "per se contrary to the Gospel."[5] He has claimed that the doctrines of Martin Luther on justification are orthodox, although they were dogmatically condemned by the Ecumenical Council of Trent,[6] and has allowed a commemorative stamp of the heresiarch to be made by the Holy See's post office.[7] His appointees have all but destroyed whole orders of priests and nuns, such as the Franciscan Friars of the Immaculate, and the Little Sisters of Mary, Mother of the Redeemer, apparently for adhering to the Church's traditional practices. He has turned over millions of Chinese Catholics to bishops

[3] See, for example, "Bishops use Pope's teaching to push homosexuality at 2018 World Meeting of Families," LifeSite, Oct. 17, 2017, at https://www.lifesitenews.com/news/bishops-use-popes-teaching-to-push-homosexuality-at-2018-world-meeting-of-f; also, "Cardinal Kasper: Homosexual unions are 'analogous' to Christian marriage," LifeSite, March 14, 2018, at https://www.lifesitenews.com/news/cardinal-kasper-homosexual-unions-are-analogous-to-christian-marriage.

[4] "Pope Francis appears to contradict, word-for-word, the doctrine of Paul VI and JPII on contraception," LifeSite, Feb. 19, 2016, at https://www.lifesitenews.com/opinion/pope-francis-appears-to-contradict-word-for-word-the-doctrine-of-paul-vi-an.

[5] "Catechism Modified," *L'Osservatore Romano,* Aug. 2, 2018, at http://www.osservatoreromano.va/en/news/death-penalty-inadmissible

[6] "Nowadays, Lutherans and Catholics, and all Protestants, are in agreement on the doctrine of justification: on this very important point he was not mistaken." See: "In-flight press conference of his Holiness Pope Francis from Armenia to Rome," Papal Flight, Sunday, 26 June 2016, at http://www.vatican.va/content/francesco/en/speeches/2016/june/documents/papa-francesco_20160626_ armenia-conferenza-stampa.html.

[7] See: "Vatican releases postage stamps on Reformation, St. Francis of Sales," *Vatican News,* Nov. 23, 2017, at https://www.vaticannews.va/en/vatican-city/news/2017-11/vatican-releases-postage-stamps-on-reformation--st--francis-of-s.html.

who are controlled by an atheistic, communist government,[8] which is in the process of shutting down Catholic parishes that refuse to accept communist state supervision.[9] Most recently, he has hosted and defended the use of images that appear to represent the earth goddess "Pachamama," while presiding over an "Amazon synod" that emphasized radical ecology and socialistic "liberation theology" over the spiritual values of the Catholic religion.[10]

The doctrinal crisis appears to be rooted in a deeper moral crisis affecting the Holy See. Francis has surrounded himself with loyalists who often appear to be ethically compromised, whose vulnerability to accusation makes them dependent on the pontiff, and who are rewarded for their sycophancy with an iron-clad impunity guaranteed by Francis himself. Those who are perceived as opponents are persecuted by applying to them an unfavorable and strict interpretation of the law, with little sign of the "mercy" Francis claims to champion. His favoritism and selective enforcement of Church law has led to an ambiance of fear among clergy and religious that facilitates his attacks on Catholic doctrine, all of which seem to be aimed at

---

[8] "Cdl Zen urges cardinals to stop the 'murder of the Church in China,'" LifeSite, Jan. 8, 2020, at https://www.lifesitenews.com/news/cdl-zen-decries-vatican-china-deal-in-letter-to-cardinals-it-disgusts-me.

[9] See the U.S. Congressional-Executive Commission on China (CECC) 2019 annual report on Freedom of Religion, at https://www.cecc.gov/sites/chinacommission.house.gov/files/documents/2019AR_FREEDOMOFRELIGION.pdf.

[10] Pope Francis defended the use of the statutes, in which he recognizes that they represent the "Pachamama" but claims there was no "idolatrous intent" in displaying them in the church of the Transpontina. See "Pope Francis announces retrieval of indigenous statues," Vatican News, Oct. 25, 2019, at https://www.vaticannews .va/en/pope/news/2019-10/pope-francis-comments-on-statues-stolen-from-church.html. Francis also was present at a ritual in which the same image was venerated and knelt before, and which he himself blessed, although he left without making his prepared remarks. See "Amazon Synod: Ecological ritual performed in Vatican gardens for pope's tree planting ceremony," *CNA*, Oct. 4, 2019, at https://www.catholicnewsagency.com/news/indigenous-ritual-performed-in-vatican-gardens-for-popes-tree-planting-ceremony-60523.

making the Catholic faith into a fashionable political ideology and to exalt Francis as a populist leader, a benevolent and permissive dictator in the mold of Argentina's Juan Perón, who is remaking the Catholic Church in his own image.[11]

The pope's more infamous protégés have included the now-defrocked ex-cardinal Theodore McCarrick, whom Francis protected and promoted, apparently despite knowing of his history of sexual predation. After a massive global outcry against McCarrick, Francis grudgingly laicized him, but not before he had promoted one of McCarrick's close associates, Cardinal Kevin Farrell, currently Prefect of the Dicastery for the Laity, Family and Life, to the position of Camerlengo of the Holy Roman Church, an appointment that will place him in administrative control of the Vatican after Francis dies or resigns.[12]

Bishop Gustavo Zanchetta, a personal favorite of Pope Francis who was personally selected by the pontiff to lead the Diocese of Orán in Argentina, was given shelter by Francis in his own residence, Casa Santa Marta, after Zanchetta fled his diocese in 2017 following highly credible accusations of sex abuse of seminarians. The accusations seem to have been ignored by the pope since he reportedly first received them in 2015,[13] although Vatican spokesman Alessandro Gisotti claimed that they had come to light only in late 2018, when a Vatican investigation of the accusations purportedly began. Zanchetta was given a

---

[11] This interpretation of the Francis papacy is made in detail and very persuasively by H. J. A. Sire (under the pen name "Marcantonio Colonna") in his work, *The Dictator Pope* (Washington, D.C.: Regnery Publishing, 2018).

[12] Farrell claims to have known nothing about McCarrick's misdeeds despite having lived with him for six years in Washington during a time when his behavior was well-known to a large number of clergy and laity. See "US Vatican cardinal: 'Not once did I even suspect' McCarrick," AP, July 31, 2018, at https://apnews.com/7d37357cb56043c89375364f46015 8a6/US-Vatican-cardinal:-"Not-once-did-I-even-suspect"-McCarrick.

[13] "Pope Francis knew of bishop's abuse years before Vatican posting, new documents indicate," LifeSite, Feb. 27, 2019, at https://www.lifesite news.com/news/pope-francis-knew-of-bishops-abuse-years-before-vatican-posting-new-documents-reveal.

special position of authority in the Vatican Bank for years following his unusual resignation until the accusations surfaced in the major media, and after a period of suspension he continues to hold his position there.[14] After dodging prosecutors for months, he has returned to Argentina multiple times to face criminal proceedings for his alleged crimes, but continues to find shelter in Casa Santa Marta with the pope when not in Argentina.[15]

Archbishop Vincenzo Paglia, who commissioned a blasphemous homoerotic mural painting of Jesus for his cathedral church before taking a Vatican position,[16] has been appointed by Pope Francis to the leadership of the St. John Paul II Pontifical Institute for Studies of Marriage and Family, as well as the Pontifical Academy for Life. He is using his position to remove large numbers of professors from the Institute who teach orthodox Catholic doctrine on marriage and family, and is rewriting the curriculum to eliminate the institute's emphasis on bioethics and moral doctrine, undermining the institute's original purpose in favor of the secularized, left-wing ideological approach of Francis.[17] He has also fired strongly pro-life mem-

---

[14] "Vatican tells Argentinian court accused bishop has job in Rome, despite being suspended," Crux, Aug. 28, 2019, at: https://cruxnow. com/vatican/2019/08/vatican-tells-argentinian-court-accused-bishop-has-job-in-rome-despite-being-suspended/.

[15] For a recent summary of the case, see: "Argentine Bishop returns to Vatican job before end of sex misconduct probe," LifeSite, June 16, 2020, at https://www.lifesitenews.com/news/argentine-bishop-returns-to-vatican-job-before-end-of-sex-misconduct-probe.

[16] "Vatican archbishop featured in homoerotic painting he commissioned," LifeSite, March 3, 2017, at https://www.lifesitenews.com/news/leading-vatican-archbishop-featured-in-homoerotic-painting-he-commissioned.

[17] A letter written recently by students of the institute asks, "Why continue to study at the John Paul II Institute if it does not seem to propose anything different from what we can find among the curricula of secular universities, usually in more attractive and effective ways?" See, "Students say changes at Rome's JPII Institute undermine its mission," *CNA*, July 26, 2019, at https://www.catholicnewsagency.com/news/stud ents-say-changes-at-romes-jpii-institute-undermine-its-mission-66538, and also, 'The term 'life' must be redefined,' new head of Vatican Life Academy

bers of the Academy and has replaced them in part with people who reject Catholic doctrine on the immorality of abortion, homosexual acts, and contraception.[18]

Other cardinals and high-ranking Vatican officials have been accused of participation in or covering up of financial and sexual scandals, including Cardinal Angelo Comastri, Vicar General of Pope Francis for Vatican City, Cardinal Francesco Coccopalmerio,[19,20] the highly-favored Substitute of the Secretariat of State Archbishop Edgar Peña Parra,[21] the Cardinal Secretary of State himself, Pietro Parolin, the former Substitute of the Secretariat of State, Cardinal Giovanni Angelo Becciu,[22] and Msgr. Battista Mario Salvatore Ricca, Prelate of the scandal-ridden Vatican Bank and Director of Casa Santa Marta, the pope's personal residence.[23]

---

declares," LifeSite, Sept. 5, 2019, at https://www.lifesitenews .com/news/the-term-life-must-be-redefined-new-head-of-vatican-life-academy-declares.

[18] See, for example: "Pro-Abortion Theologian Picked as Pontifical Academy for Life Member," *National Catholic Register,* June 13, 2017, at https://www.ncregister.com/daily-news/pro-abortion-theologian-picked-as-pontifical-academy-for-life-member.

[19] See, for example, "New Viganò testimony: Vatican covered up allegations of sexual abuse of Pope's altar boys," LifeSite, July 3, 2019, at https://www.lifesitenews.com/news/new-vigano-testimony-vatican-covered-up-allegations-of-sexual-abuse-of-popes-altar-boys.

[20] "Source: Vatican cardinal was at drug-fueled homosexual party, and Pope knows it," LifeSite, Oct. 10, 2018, at https://www.lifesitenews.com /news/source-vatican-cardinal-was-at-drug-fueled-homosexual-party-and-pope-knows.

[21] "New Viganò testimony," op. cit.

[22] Becciu recently resigned from the cardinalate following an investigation of various suspicious financial transactions in which he was involved. Peña Parra and Parolin, together with Becciu, have been the subjects of multiple articles in local Italian and other media regarding allegations of malfeasance involving apparently illegal investments of millions of dollars of Vatican money through shady middlemen, which has led to raids on the office of the Secretariat of State by Vatican police.

[23] The Ricca appointment was maintained by Pope Francis despite a detailed report by Sandro Magister in the Italian newspaper *L'Espresso* of repeated homosexual misbehavior on the part of the priest while he was a member of the Vatican diplomatic corps. The Vatican issued a statement

Cardinal Maradiaga: at the pinnacle of power

However, in this disturbing array of questionable appointments, one prelate stands out both for his blackened reputation and his powerful influence over the pope. Cardinal Óscar Andrés Rodríguez Maradiaga, Archbishop of Tegucigalpa, Honduras, is, after Pope Francis, the most influential prelate in the Catholic Church today, so much so that he has been dubbed the "Vice Pope," by the Italian media. He is the pope's most intimate collaborator and highest-ranked counselor among the cardinals, holding the title of Coordinator of Francis' elite Council of Cardinal Advisers. In virtue of his office, he is also the chief architect of Francis' reform for the Holy See, and therefore, by extension, the Catholic Church as a whole. Until 2015 he led Caritas Internationalis, which oversees the Catholic Church's massive expenditures on "international development." Maradiaga was also deeply influential in Francis' election to the papacy, and is believed to have personally convinced Jorge Bergoglio to accept the office, a fact that is corroborated by Martha Alegría Reichmann in *Sacred Betrayals*.

Like so many of Pope Francis' closest associates, Maradiaga's name is associated not only with power, but with tyrannical rule, personal corruption, and the unconditional defense of his powerful patron. Maradiaga is widely accused of ruling his archdiocese as a self-serving dictator who destroys the priestly careers of those who fall out of his favor, particularly those who dare to object to the personal misconduct of his (now former) auxiliary bishop and protégé, Juan José Pineda Fasquelle. A series of moral and financial scandals have all but ruined Maradiaga's public reputation, both in Honduras and abroad, and his alliance with the oppressive power structure in his own country has made him so infamous that he must be protected

---

that did not deny the report but called it "not credible," and Francis later said that he ordered a "brief investigation" that "found nothing."

from attacks[24] by those protesting the ruling regime, and he is met with insults from the public on the few occasions that he dares to venture into the street.[25] In this way Maradiaga shares much in common with Pope Francis, who also occupied the most important see in his country before his election to the papacy, was also allied with the country's power structure, and also dealt harshly with those perceived as having crossed him.

Maradiaga exposed: the beginning of the scandal

Although Maradiaga's reputation for abusive misrule within his archdiocese dates back decades, his exposure in the Honduran press began in June of 2016, when Maradiaga suddenly resigned from the presidency of the country's episcopal conference, claiming he had to focus on Pope Francis' curial reform project.

In July, an anonymous group of priests and laymen "committed to cleaning up the Church and the Catholic University of Honduras" issued a multi-page declaration accusing Maradiaga and his auxiliary bishop, Juan José Pineda, of embezzling large quantities of funds from the Catholic University of Honduras, for which they were acting as Grand Chancellor and Deputy Grand Chancellor. The authors claimed that the withdrawals of money amounted to half a million dollars per year, with the

[24] Edward Pentin, Rome Correspondent for the *National Catholic Register*, tweeted the following on May 30, 2019: "++Maradiaga has been evacuated from a Rome-bound plane due to political protests at Honduras airport. Sources say he was led out the back of the airport, across runway, due to danger of lynching. His support for govt's bad policies means he's seen as paid govt official, they say." See: https://twitter.com/edwardpentin/status/1134175267814027265.

[25] The Honduran radio station Radio América HN tweeted the following on Dec. 10, 2019: "The archbishop of Tegucigalpa, Óscar Andrés Rodríguez [Maradiaga], told the program Doble Vía that he doesn't go out onto the street with much frequency, but he has done so and has received insults, [saying] 'Poor people, they will have to give an accounting to God.'" See: https://mobile.twitter.com/radioamericahn/status/12045513 57920948225.

connivance of the university's rector, Elio Alvarenga Amado, who was hiding the transfers with a double accounting system. Simultaneously the university administration was accused of purging the university's ranks of its most eminent and important founding professors and administrators, while Maradiaga sent priests into exile for falling afoul of Pineda, whose "homosexuality and abuse of others" were "widely known."

The letter indicated that complaints of the misconduct of Maradiaga and Pineda had been made to the apostolic nuncio, Archbishop Luigi Bianco, but that they had been ignored, and expressed hope that the then-current apostolic nuncio, the African archbishop Novatus Rugambwa, would be more open to hearing the testimony of those who had been damaged by the misconduct of the cardinal and his auxiliary. It also stated that the other bishops of Honduras were aware of the embezzlement, and that Cardinal Maradiaga had been forced to relinquish the leadership of the country's episcopal conference as a result.

The declaration was published by one of Honduras' few truly independent publications, the internet news service Confidencial Honduras, in July of 2016, and the article is reprinted in full in the appendix of this book.[26] The Archdiocese of Tegucigalpa and the University of Honduras both issued vague denials regarding the money transfers, claiming merely that no laws or university rules had been violated, and threatening legal action for institutional "defamation." The claim that Maradiaga had been forced out of the presidency of the episcopal conference was deflected by claiming that he was merely anticipating his mandatory resignation at the age of 75.[27] Only a single individual bishop, an

[26] "Corrupción en Universidad católica orilló caída de cardenal Rodríguez," Confidencial Honduras, July 28, 2016 (translation provided in in the appendix of this book), at https://confidencialhn.com/corrupcion-en-universidad-catolica-orillo-caida-de-cardenal-rodriguez/.

[27] The response of the Archdiocese of Tegucigalpa can be found at https://tiempo.hn/wp-content/uploads/2016/07/arqui1.jpg1(p.1), and https://tiempo.hn/wp-content/uploads/2016/07/arqui2.jpg (p.2). The response of the Catholic University of Honduras can be found at

auxiliary from the diocese of San Pedro Sula, wrote to deny that Maradiaga had been forced to resign, although the reasons he gave for his resignation were different from those offered by Maradiaga and his proxies.[28]

Cardinal Maradiaga responded to this reporting by filing a legal complaint against Confidencial Honduras, but was unable to proceed because the publication had ample proof of its claims. However, coverage of the story in Honduras began to diminish and there was little further investigation by the local press.

Francis shelves investigation, defends Maradiaga

Although the story had mostly disappeared from the Honduran media, the wheels of Vatican justice were moving under the impetus of Archbishop Rugambwa, who was committed to carrying out his duty of reporting complaints to the Holy See despite pressure to the contrary by Maradiaga and Pineda. His reports resulted in the launching of a formal investigation led by an apostolic visitor, the Argentinean bishop Jorge Pedro Casaretto, who came to Honduras in May of 2017 to collect personal testimony and documentation on the case.

Soon after, Pope Francis received an extensive dossier of the scandal from Casaretto supported by interviews by approximately 50 witnesses, which were later reported to include "humble priests saying mass in isolated parishes in the forests of Honduras, seminarians, lay employees, even elderly widows and former friends of the cardinal."[29] The testimony corrobo-

---

https://tiempo.hn/wp-content/uploads/2016/07/unicah.jpg (p.1), and https://tiempo.hn/wp-content/uploads/2016/07/unicah2.jpg (p.2).

[28] Emiliani, Rómulo. "¿Por qué atacar al Cardenal?" *El Heraldo,* Aug. 9, 2016, at https://www.elheraldo.hn/opinion/columnas/98988 2-469/por-qué-atacar-al-cardenal.

[29] This would later be reported by Emiliano Fittipaldi in his article, "El lado oscuro de Maradiaga," *L'Espresso,* Feb. 5, 2018, at http://espresso.repubblica.it/inchieste/2018/02/05/news/el-lado-oscuro-de-maradiaga-1.317878.

rated the original 2016 accusations, indicating that Maradiaga was siphoning off over half a million dollars a year from the university and that substantial funds, perhaps millions of dollars, were finding their way into the hands of Pineda. Testimony also indicated that the Pineda had also received a massive grant from the Honduran government of the equivalent of 1.3 million USD for the benefit of Catholic Church projects serving the poor, and that no receipts existed to prove the funds had been used for such purposes.

Later reporting by Edward Pentin of the National Catholic Register would indicate that Pineda was living a very lavish lifestyle, which included multiple first class flights to Spain to visit "close male friends," and the ownership of several expensive cars.[30] Millions of dollars in unaccounted-for money appeared to have been entrusted to an obscure investment firm called "Leman Wealth Management" that had mysteriously disappeared, along with at least some of the funds.

Reports were also made to Casaretto about a layman who dressed as a priest named Erick Cravioto Farjado, who enjoyed an apparently homosexual relationship with Pineda, and who was living in Villa Iris, the archbishop's residence, with both Pineda and Maradiaga. Eventually, Cravioto had moved out of Villa Iris but had been given an apartment and a car by Pineda, with funds that were believed to be taken from the university or some other ecclesiastical source.

Pope Francis was reportedly shocked by the dossier, and announced that he would be deciding the case himself. However, it appears that the pontiff did nothing and simply shelved the case. After half a year of inaction by Francis, the existence of the dossier and its contents were leaked to the Italian investigative journalist Emiliano Fittipaldi, who published an exposé of the case in the magazine L'Espresso in late December of

[30] "Still No Action Taken Against Honduran Bishop Accused of Sexual Abuse," *National Catholic Register*, Apr. 27, 2018, at https://www.ncregister.com/blog/edward-pentin/still-no-action-taken-against-honduran-bishop-accused-of-sexual-abuse.

2017, one that included a broad account of the affair, including the pope's private reaction.[31] In early 2018, *L'Espresso* also published images of accounting documents proving its case.[32] For the first time, the scandal had become international news.

Cardinal Maradiaga responded by admitting that he had received the quantities of money reported by Fittipaldi, but claimed that the funds were used for various Church and charitable expenses,[33] an assertion for which he has never provided evidence. He claimed that "the funds are not managed in my name, but rather in the name of the Archdiocese,"[34] an affirmation that would soon be refuted by the archdiocesan accounting documents published by *L'Espresso*. He gave a firm but somewhat ambiguous denial regarding his purported investments in "Leman Wealth Management," claiming that "the archdiocesan economic council has never authorized this type of investment," and added, "Regarding me, I don't even know if in London there is a financial company with that name."[35]

In addition, Maradiaga attacked Fittipaldi personally, calling him an "unethical reporter, doomed to fail, who earns money with infamous books" and suggested that the leaks to the press were a maneuver by enemies being used to force him out of office, as he was about to reach the age at which Church law requires him to offer his resignation to the pope.[36] His enemies, according to Maradiaga, are "people opposed to the reform of the Vatican Curia who want to slander me to make me leave the service of Mother Church and the Holy Father Fran-

[31] "L'ultimo scandalo Vaticano: 35 mila euro al mese per il cardinale Maradiaga," *L'Espresso*, Dec. 26, 2017, at http://espresso.repubblica it/in chieste/2017/12/26/news/l-ultimo-scandalo-vaticano-35-mila-euro-al-mese-per-il-cardinale-maradiaga-1.316467.

[32] "El lado oscuro de Maradiaga," *op. cit.*

[33] "Cardenal Rodríguez Maradiaga responde a acusaciones de revista italiana," *CNA*, Dec. 22, 2017, at https://www.aciprensa.com/noticias/cardenal-rodriguez-maradiaga-responde-a-acusaciones-de-revista-italiana-74083.

[34] Ibid.

[35] "El lado oscuro de Maradiaga," *op. cit.*

[36] Ibid.

cis."[37] This last claim would become a standard one in Maradiaga's arsenal of counterattacks against journalists who reported unflattering news about him.

Finally, Pope Francis himself came to Maradiaga's defense. Vatican News, an official news organ of the Holy See, reported a radio interview with the cardinal following a private conversation with Francis, in which Maradiaga quoted the pope as saying, "I'm pained by the evil that they have done to you, but don't worry about it," with the second part of the quote in the headline itself.[38] In January of 2018, a Honduran publication reported that the pope would not be accepting Maradiaga's mandatory resignation, submitted at the end of the previous year.[39]

In February of 2018, *L'Espresso* responded to Maradiaga's attacks, noting that accounting documentation submitted by the Archdiocese of Tegucigalpa to the Vatican's apostolic visitor (and published by *L'Espresso*) showed no indication that the vast funds taken by the cardinal had ever been deposited in the archdiocese's bank accounts. They also showed no evidence that over one million dollars given to Bishop Pineda by the Honduran government for Church expenses had ever been deposited with the archdiocese or had ever been spent on Church-related projects. The funds seemed to have simply disappeared from the account in which they had originally been deposited.[40]

---

[37] "Cardenal Rodríguez Maradiaga responde a acusaciones . . ." *op. cit.*
[38] "S.E. Cardenal Rodríguez Maradiaga: el Papa me dijo 'no te preocupes,'" *Vatican News,* Dec. 26, 2017, at https://www.vaticannews.va/es/iglesia/news/2017-12/s-e-cardenal-rodriguez-maradiaga--el-papa-me-dijo--no-te-preocu.html.
[39] "Papa Francisco no habría aceptado dimisión del cardenal Óscar Rodríguez como arzobispo de Tegucigalpa," *El Heraldo,* Jan. 3, 2018, at https://www.elheraldo.hn/pais/1140148-466/papa-francisco-no-habría-aceptado-dimisión-del-cardenal-Óscar-rodríguez-como-arzobispo
[40] "El lado oscuro de Maradiaga," *op. cit.*

"Epidemic" of homosexuality in seminary where Pineda is accused of sexual abuse

The revelations about Rodríguez Maradiaga and Pineda Fasquelle took an even darker turn in March of 2018, when the Rome correspondent of the *National Catholic Register*, Edward Pentin, revealed that Bishop Pineda had been accused by two seminarians of having sexually abused seminary students, in testimony submitted to Bishop Casaretto in May of 2017. Pentin also revealed allegations of Pineda maintaining homosexual relationships with a number of individuals besides the pseudo-priest Erick Cravioto Farjado, including another non-ordained "priest" who functioned fraudulently as a Catholic police chaplain with the blessing of Cardinal Maradiaga. The accusations were even more serious given the fact that Pineda was not only an auxiliary bishop in the archdiocese, but at different times was head of the seminary itself, as well as Vicar General of the archdiocese and the head of the archdiocesan ecclesiastical tribunal.[41]

In April, Pentin reported that Archbishop Pineda was continuing in his position as Auxiliary Bishop of Tegucigalpa with impunity, nine months after the pope had received the Casaretto dossier containing testimony of Pineda's acts of sexual abuse of seminarians and homosexual trysts. Pineda was being left in charge of the archdiocese for weeks at a time while Cardinal Maradiaga was away. "Everything is kept silent and so everything continues as it always has," Pentin was told by one of his sources. Unfortunately, nothing has changed, only threats have been made against those who have revealed themselves." Another source told Pentin that "everything is the same" and that

---

[41] "Former Seminarians Allege Grave Sexual Misconduct by Honduran Bishop Pineda," *National Catholic Register,* March 4, 2018, at http://www.ncregister.com/daily-news/former-seminarians-allege-grave-sexual-misconduct-by-honduran-bishop-pineda

"Pineda remains in his position with the protection of Maradiaga."[42]

In June a group of 48 seminarians out of 180 of the total at the Major Seminary of Tegucigalpa issued an open letter to Cardinal Maradiaga and the bishops of Honduras in general, complaining of an "epidemic" of homosexual sodomy in the seminary. Edward Pentin would later report that Cardinal Maradiaga had attacked the seminarians who wrote the letter, calling them "gossipers" seeking to make fellow seminarians look bad. According to one source that spoke to Pentin, Maradiaga had long refused to acknowledge the problem, which was so bad that "some formators recently refused to participate in priestly ordinations because of the candidates' alleged homosexuality," in Pentin's words. The source then added, "The cardinal ordained them himself." Maradiaga and the President of the Honduran Bishops' Conference, Angel Garachana Pérez, immediately began to denounce the authors of the letter when it was read at a meeting of the Honduran bishops, reported Pentin.[43]

In July, Pentin's article documenting the contents of the open letter appeared in the *National Catholic Register.* The Honduran Episcopal Conference leadership, now under the authority of Maradiaga's successor and ally Bishop Angel Garachana Pérez, issued an ambiguous statement published by the Holy See's Vatican News, claiming that there was no "institutional" homosexual misbehavior in the seminary, while admitting vaguely the existence of "affective and sexual weakness" that can "generate inadequate attitudes and behaviors." However, Garachana condemned Pentin's report and the seminarians who had written the public letter, referring to their act of

---

[42] "Still No Action Taken Against Honduran Bishop Accused of Sexual Abuse," *op. cit.*
[43] "Honduran Seminarians Allege Widespread Homosexual Misconduct," *National Catholic Register,* July 25, 2018, at http://www.ncreg ister.com/daily-news/honduran-seminarians-allege-widespread-homosexual-misconduct.

exposing the scandal as an example of "weeds and evil" in the Church.[44] Meanwhile, Pentin reported, the Honduran bishops were investigating the charges made in the letter, a fact acknowledged by Bishop Guy Charbonneau of Choluteca.[45]

Cardinal Maradiaga, however, resisted any reform of the seminary. In early August, Edward Pentin issued a tweeted update on the affair: "Latest word from Honduras: All homosexual seminarians have been sent away except those in Tegucigalpa archdiocese who joke they have a very strong and powpowerful 'patron saint': ++Maradiaga. The cardinal has 'again used his weight to break rules and agreements with other bishops.'" Pentin additionally told LifeSite that his sources believed that "about 40 seminarians [out of a total of 180 in the Tegucigalpa seminary] are actively homosexual, and about 20 more are in the closet. Many repress it to be able to reach ordination but once ordained, they are 'free and unbridled.'"[46]

Pineda resigns, and Francis continues to defend Maradiaga

It was also in July, a few days before the publication of Pentin's stories on the epidemic of homosexual activity in the seminary, that Pope Francis suddenly accepted Bishop Pineda's resignation, which the archdiocese later claimed had been tendered by Pineda in 2017. Pineda was no longer Tegucigalpa's auxiliary bishop. No reasons were given publicly for the resignation; Pineda wrote a public letter cryptically stating that

---

[44] "Honduras: En el Seminario Mayor existe un ambiente que sigue moral y normas de la Iglesia," *Vatican News*, July 30, 2018, at https://www.vaticannews.va/es/iglesia/news/2018-07/honduras-iglesia-papa-francisco-cardenal-rodriguez-maradiaga.html.

[45] "Honduran Seminarians Allege Widespread Homosexual Misconduct," *op. cit.*

[46] "Report: Cardinal close to Pope is protecting cadre of gay seminarians in Honduras," LifeSite, Aug. 8, 2018, at https://www.lifesitenews.com/news/report-cardinal-close-to-pope-is-protecting-cadre-of-gay-seminarians-in-hon.

"God and my superiors know the reasons and motives" for his resignation. "I have tried, with all of my heart, to serve this portion of the People of God," he wrote, adding, "If I succeeded, blessed be God, if I failed them, I ask for forgiveness."[47] The bishop subsequently gave an interview to Tegucigalpa's Channel 5 television station in which he referred vaguely to unspecified accusations against him, calling them "absolutely false," and claiming that the pope had told him he would continue "being a missionary, priest, and bishop." "What's happening is that you are no longer, because you have requested it, the auxiliary bishop of the Archdiocese of Tegucigalpa," he quoted the pope as saying.[48] He was given the honorable title "Auxiliary Bishop Emeritus of Tegucigalpa," and appeared to be unhindered by any penalty. His whereabouts are currently unknown to the public.

Despite the sympathetic treatment he was receiving from Pope Francis, Maradiaga was now feeling the pain of his increasingly ruined international reputation. He gave his customary response to negative coverage, portraying himself as a victim and attacking Pentin personally, as he had Fittipaldi, claiming that Pentin was seeking to attack Pope Francis and derail his reform of the Vatican. "For three years I have been the victim of a 'hit man' who practices media harassment," Maradiaga told Periodista Digital. "His name is Edward Pentin and he works for an EWTN newspaper that is called the 'National Catholic Register.' I have never spoken to him, but he has availed himself of an 'anonymous libel' that was published

---

[47] "Juan José Pineda tras renuncia aceptada por el papa Francisco: 'Si les fallé, pido perdón,'" *El Heraldo*, July 20, 2018, at https://www.elheraldo.hn/pais/1199462-469/juan-josé-pineda-tras-renuncia-aceptada-por-el-papa-francisco-si-les.

[48] The interview was later reported on and quoted extensively by *Periodista Digital*. See, "Juan José Pineda niega haber cometido irregularidades o haber tenido mala conducta," *Periodista Digital*, July 22, 2018, at https://www.periodistadigital.com/cultura/religion/america/201 80722/juan-jose-pineda-niega-haber-cometido-irregularidades-o-haber-tenido-mala-conducta-noticia-689401443669/.

by another Honduran 'hit man' through local media who insults me constantly and defames me."[49]

He added: "Clearly the only motive is because I am the Coordinator of the Council of Cardinals that is working on the reform of the Vatican Curia. The enemies of this reform want to do away with this council. The principal object is Pope Francis."[50] In September he complained publicly of "fecal networks" spreading lies about him.[51] Later that same month, speaking privately to archdiocesan clergy, he complained, "The devil is striking me from every side."[52]

Pope Francis seemed to agree. Many months later, in May of 2019, Francis was continuing to support Maradiaga, and made it clear that he had discarded the testimonies against him for lack of evidence, calling them "calumnies." "Oh well, they say things about the poor man all over the place, but nothing has been proved," he told Valentina Alazraki of Televisa. "No, in that respect he's honest, and I took care to investigate things. They're calumnies. No one could prove anything to me. He

---

[49] Pentin wrote in response that it was "very sad and regrettable that the cardinal should choose to launch this attack rather than deal with the very serious issues relating to the Church in Honduras on which I've reported, and which he has still yet to answer." Pentin stated that he had written to the cardinal "four times" asking him to comment on all the accusations against him so he could "give his side of the story" and added that he also offered to meet the cardinal while he was in Rome. "All of these requests were never answered," Pentin said. See "Cardinal Maradiaga blames 'hit man' journalist for allegations against him," *Catholic Herald,* Aug. 30, 2018 at https://catholicherald.co.uk/embattled-cardinal-maradiaga-says-he-is-the-victim-of-journalist-hit-man/.

[50] "Maradiaga: 'Soy víctima de un 'sicario' que se llama Edward Pentin,'" *Periodista Digital,* Aug. 29, 2018, at https://www.periodistadigital.com/cultura/religion/america/20180829/maradiaga-victima-sicario-llama-edward-pentin-noticia-689401624066/.

[51] See, "Cardenal hondureño califica a las redes sociales de 'redes fecales,'" *El Nuevo Herald,* Sept. 2, 2018, at https://www.elnuevoherald.com/noticias/mundo/america-latina/article217740430.html.

[52] Recorded conversation reported in, "Maradiaga se lamenta con sus curas: 'De todos lados me pega el demonio,'" *InfoVaticana,* Sept. 13, 2018, at https://infovaticana.com/2018/09/13/maradiaga-se-lamenta-con-sus-curas-de-todos-lados-me-pega-el-demonio/.

made some mistakes, but not on the level that they want to claim. That's important, so in this I defend him."[53]

Francis' words, which appeared to dismiss the testimony of dozens of witnesses, were similar to those he had used in January of 2018 when he infamously defended Chilean bishop Juan Barros Madrid, an appointee of Francis who was credibly accused of sex abuse cover-ups. On that occasion Francis also called the accusations against Barros "calumny" and claimed that no evidence existed to verify them, despite testimony from multiple victims, some of which had been submitted directly to him by the archbishop of Boston, Cardinal Seán O'Malley. Francis was ultimately forced by public pressure to retract his statements, apologize, and remove Barros from office, a fate that is yet to befall Francis' "vice pope." Instead, Maradiaga was reaffirmed as the Coordinator of the Council of Cardinal Advisers in October of 2020.

Enter Martha Alegría Reichmann de Valladares

Emiliano Fittipaldi's investigations had led him also to an unlikely source of information on the cardinal's misdeeds: Martha Alegría Reichmann de Valladares, wife of the now-deceased former ambassador of Honduras to the Holy See and former Dean of the Vatican diplomatic corps, Alejandro Emilio Valladares Lanza.

Alegría Reichmann was and is the most intimate insider in the story of Maradiaga's saga of corrupt power politics. For almost four decades she and her husband had been the cardinal's closest personal friends, and he had resided in their home in Rome whenever he had visited the city. Valladares had been Maradiaga's most loyal advocate in the Vatican, pushing relentlessly for his nomination as cardinal until it was achieved, which made Maradiaga the first Honduran cardinal in history.

[53] "Entrevista exclusiva con el Papa Francisco; Valentina Alazraki entrevista al Papa Francisco," *Televisa,* May 31, 2019, posted on YouTube at https://www.youtube.com/watch?v=VOcLWcW6Elw.

The couple had also become close friends with Fr. Juan José Pineda Fasquelle, an intimate associate of Maradiaga who would eventually be named as his auxiliary bishop in Tegucigalpa.

In their decades of service together in Rome, Valladares and Alegría Reichmann had developed friendships with much of the Vatican curia, including the Cardinal Secretary of State Pietro Parolin, who eulogized Vallardes in his homily at Valladares' requiem mass in December 2013 in Rome.[54] The couple had made the acquaintance of Pope John Paul II, Pope Benedict, and Pope Francis as well. Alegría was the author of two books of spiritual poetry and narrative, one of which was published by the Vatican in 2013,[55] and her paintings had been displayed in exhibitions worldwide and even reproduced on postage stamps.

Fittipaldi learned from his sources that the couple's relationship with Cardinal Maradiaga and his auxiliary bishop had soured after Maradiaga had convinced the couple to invest their money in "Leman Wealth Management," the same organization that had reportedly disappeared with millions of dollars in archdiocesan funds. The two had lost most of their life savings in the swindle, and Alegría Reichmann, now a widow, had filed a complaint with the Vatican for Maradiaga's "fraudulent mediation."

Although Alegría refused to talk to Fittipaldi when he first published an article on her case in February 2018,[56] she later agreed to an exclusive interview with the Italian journalist in

---

[54] "Celebrazione Eucaristica in suffragio dell'amabsciatore Alejandro Emilio Valladares Lanza," Dec. 2, 2013, at http://www.vatican.va/roman _curia/secretariat_state/parolin/2013/documents/rc_seg-st_ 20131202_ suffragio-amb-lanza_it.html.

[55] That is, *Yo te encontré* (Rome: Librería Editorial Vaticano, 2013).

[56] "La vedova attacca il cardinale Maradiaga: frodata per colpa sua, ho perso tutti i soldi," *L'Espresso*, Feb. 5, 2018, at http://espresso.repubb lica.it/inchieste/2018/02/05/news/maradiaga-conti-dubbi-1.317885.

early March of the same year,[57] followed by an interview in late May with Edward Pentin.[58] What she revealed to the two reporters was startling: Maradiaga had induced his closest friends, a couple he claimed to regard as members of his own family, to place their savings in a bogus, fly-by-night investment scheme whose integrity and security he had personally vouched for. When the family's fortune disappeared, Maradiaga disappeared from their lives as well, conceding only a brief meeting in which he offered no explanation for the loss of her money but offering her a fraction of her losses in an apparent attempt to purchase her silence.

From that day on he dodged all attempts by the now-widowed Alegría to communicate with him. When, after months of seeking another audience with the cardinal she finally cornered him in the archdiocesan cathedral, he had instructed her to hide his own involvement in the affair and blame another individual for her loss, refusing to help her recover her money, join in a lawsuit or other legal action, or to identify himself with the case in any way. From that point on, Maradiaga refused all contact with Alegría.

Alegría's allegations about Maradiaga's relationship with Bishop Pineda were disturbing as well. She told Pentin that there are "many victims" of Cardinal Maradiaga, "and the common factor is that we have all had some problem with Auxiliary Bishop Juan Pineda. It is clear to us that anyone who touches Pineda is condemned by Rodríguez [Maradiaga]." She added: "It is known that at present the Church in Tegucigalpa is governed by terror towards anyone who dares to question the cardinal's bad decisions or, even more dangerously, to rub

---

[57] "«Ingannati e traditi, mi hanno rubato tutto». Le accuse contro il braccio destro del papa," *L'Espresso,* Mar. 2, 2018, at http://espresso.repubblica.it/inchieste/2018/03/02/news/ingannati-e-traditi-mi-hanno-rubato-tutto-le-accuse-contro-il-braccio-destro-del-papa-1.319034.

[58] "Former Honduran Ambassador's Wife Speaks of Cardinal's Alleged Role in Mismanaged Fund," *National Catholic Register,* May 22, 2018, at http://www.ncregister.com/blog/edward-pentin/diocese-recommend-investor-accused-of-taking-widows-life-savings.

up against the auxiliary [bishop] Juan Jose Pineda. Everyone who has done this has already been marginalized."

Finally, Alegría revealed that she had taken her case against Maradiaga and Pineda to Pope Francis himself, who had promised her justice, but still had yet to act. Nonetheless, she had not given up hope. "I hope that the pope will help me. He greeted me with comforting words, promising me that I would have justice. He spoke to me like a father full of love."

Sacred Betrayals opens window into life of Rodríguez Maradiaga

The groundbreaking interviews, which were quoted widely in the international secular and Catholic press, provided further evidence of Maradiaga's corruption and ruthless cruelty, but did nothing to spur Pope Francis to correct his wayward protégé. It appeared that Pope Francis had, despite his encouraging words, shelved Alegría's case along with the numerous other complaints against both Maradiaga and Pineda.

After several failed attempts to obtain a response to her complaint, Alegría Reichmann realized that Pope Francis himself was either unable or unwilling to correct the misdeeds of his "vice pope," who seemed to enjoy absolute impunity under the pope's protection. Moreover, she began to recognize that she was only one of many victims of Maradiaga's cynical regime in Tegucigalpa, the cruelty of which she herself had too easily overlooked while she and her husband enjoyed the cardinal's friendship. She resolved to write a full-length exposé of her experiences at the hand of Maradiaga and ultimately Francis himself, in order to alert the public to the corruption and abuses being committed at the highest levels of the Church against many priests and laity, who were being systematically robbed of their contributions to the Church.

Her book, which recounts the "sacred betrayals" committed against her family and other Honduran Catholics by Maradiaga, Pineda, and ultimately Pope Francis, was published in

Honduras in February of 2019. Although it was widely read and discussed in Honduras, it was ignored by most of the country's media, which is owned by and serves the oligarchic establishment that controls the country and to which Maradiaga is allied. Only Confidencial Honduras, an internet news service that dissents from the party line, as well as its now-defunct radio station Radio Globo, the internet news service Criterio.hn, the newspaper *El Libertador*, and several eminent blogs, were willing to cover Alegría's allegations against Maradiaga and Pope Francis.

Alegría's account opens a unique and privileged window into the inner workings of the administration of the pope's most powerful lieutenant, and what it reveals should stir the consciences of all faithful Catholics. It illustrates the troubling relationship between personal sexual immorality, financial malfeasance, and selective impunity at the highest levels of Church leadership. It also contains numerous revelations and descriptions that illustrate the depth of corruption of the man Pope Francis has chosen as the public face of his reform project, and who mysteriously continues to occupy his position despite the massive scandals that have engulfed him since 2016.

Sacred Betrayals reveals that Rodríguez Maradiaga regarded Pope Francis as indebted to him for his election and for convincing him to accept the papacy, suggesting that even Francis cannot control the cardinal, who seems exempt from any accountability for his personal misbehavior and abuse of power. The book also sheds light on what Alegría calls the "excessive" and "unhealthy" relationship between the cardinal and his close friend and later auxiliary bishop, who was housed with Rodríguez Maradiaga for years in the archbishop's residence of Villa Iris – along with Bishop Pineda's close male friend, a layman who was passed off as a priest.

According to Alegría, Rodríguez Maradiaga destroyed the careers of many priests and severed friendships over objections to Pineda's scandalous behavior, behavior that even gave rise to accusations of sexual predation of seminarians, and eventually led to the auxiliary's forced resignation in 2018. Moreover, she believes that she herself fell afoul of the cardinal in part because of her own objections to Pineda's conduct. Alegría recounts that Maradiaga attempted to silence her regarding Pineda and even to induce her to lie to protect himself, leading her to a rude awakening regarding his true character.

Sacred Betrayals gives the perspective of one of Cardinal Maradiaga's closest friends, the wife of an eminent diplomat who for decades shared her home with the prelate, experiencing some of the most important and private moments of his ecclesiastical career, and yet became a major victim of his deceptions and abuse of power. It also illustrates the connection between the crisis of clerical homosexuality and financial corruption, following a trail of malfeasance that leads to the personal residence of the cardinal and the scandalous behavior of his closest associates.

Perhaps most importantly, the book sheds light on the involvement of Pope Francis, who has refused justice to Alegría Reichmann and her family, and has openly defended Maradiaga, while granting virtual impunity to Bishop Pineda, ultimately accepting his resignation as auxiliary bishop only after his hand was forced by media pressure. To this day, Pineda remains uncensured by the pope for his alleged offenses, which include multiple reported allegations of sex abuse. His whereabouts are unknown.

The whereabouts of Youssry Henien, the reputed swindler who appears to have disappeared with millions of dollars of archdiocesan funds as well as the savings of the Valladares family and other Hondurans, are also unknown. It appears that finding Henien may be the only way to resolve the fate of the lost money, and to determine Maradiaga's real motives in investing in his fly-by-night scheme. However, following multiple accusations of fraud and malfeasance committed in different parts of the world and the opening and closing of many limited liability companies by Henien and his associates, he remains at large.

Sacred Betrayals is a story not only of the betrayal of a friend and the mistreatment of a widow, but is also about the abuse of an entire archdiocese by the most influential of the pope's cardinals, apparently under the protection of the pope himself. It represents an important cry for justice against the regime of cynicism, corruption, and impunity that have characterized the Francis regime, and has done grave harm to the reputation of the Catholic Church. As such, it is of vital importance to the cause of ecclesiastical reform.

I have spent many months working closely with Martha Alegría on this English edition of her book, translating the work, adding footnotes, and working with Martha to adapt the text to an international English-speaking audience. I have been deeply moved by the hurt she has experienced at the hands of Catholic prelates, but also by her bravery, and her firm resolution to seek justice and accountability from the Church's highest authorities. In her own particular way, Martha has suffered terribly from the corruption that infects the Church, both in Honduras and in Rome. Although she is now widowed and personally in a position of weakness, she has refused to remain silent, trusting in the strength of God for the vindication of her cause, which is not merely her own, but ultimately that of the whole Catholic Church. It is my hope that this book will contribute to authentic reform of this divine institution, so that it may rise again from the ruin of scandal and corruption, and shine clearly as the "light of the world" that Christ established it to be.

CHAPTER I

A PROFOUND FRIENDSHIP

In Rome

In 1991 my husband, Alejandro Emilio Valladares Lanza, was appointed ambassador of our country, Honduras, to the Holy See. As a result, we moved to Rome that same year with our two daughters, Sofia (17) and Rocío (13). Two months later, a young priest of the Order of the Claretians who was finishing his studies of Canon Law in Rome visited us at home, introducing himself as Juan José Pineda Fasquelle, having been recommended to us by our great friend, the then Msgr. Óscar Andrés Rodríguez Maradiaga.[59] We had made his acquaintance a few years after Alejandro and I had married, around 1979, when Maradiaga was the auxiliary bishop of Tegucigalpa. He and my husband got along splendidly and had a great affinity for one another.

Monsignor Rodríguez Maradiaga visited us every year on December 24, no matter the time, but he was never absent from our home for long. We have photos with him and with our daughters from those years. He gave our daughters First Com-

---

[59] Although "Maradiaga" is the maternal last name of the cardinal, and normally in Spanish-speaking countries people are known by their paternal last name (in this case, "Rodríguez") or both last names together, in general Martha follows the international convention of referring to the cardinal using his maternal last name, "Maradiaga," or both last names together ("Rodríguez Maradiaga").

munion and was present at many of our celebrations as well as our moments of difficulty and suffering.

My husband had many priest friends and loved to converse with them. Alejandro was a man of the Church, coherent and very solid in his faith, inclined to prayer, and impressively well-educated in matters of religion. Sometimes I would tell him that he was a frustrated priest, that he couldn't give me a good explanation of why he had not decided for the priesthood instead of marriage.

Before his appointment as ambassador, Alejandro had worked as general manager in a cinema company, but when Mrs. Enriqueta de Lázarus, the last surviving founding partner, died at the age of one hundred, Alejandro began to have problems because certain members of the Lázarus family were seeking to seize control of the company from other inheritors, and Alejandro's honest administration was hindering them.

They began to make his life difficult. They ordered an audit and found that everything was perfectly in order. Unsatisfied, they ordered a second audit from a different company and received the same result. So they had no choice but to seek to discredit Alejandro while violating his rights as an employee, for which Alejandro filed a lawsuit and easily won. However, they appealed and extended the litigation for seven years.

It is important to clarify that it was only a branch of the Lázarus family that was determined to sink Alejandro and to discredit him; a woman from that part of the family sought, among others, our friend, the then young Monsignor Rodríguez Maradiaga, to discredit us with him, but he ordered his secretary to tell her that if she wanted him to speak badly of Alejandro, she shouldn't bother to come because he would not receive her. My husband thanked him for that attitude all his life and used to say, "The cardinal has always been with us, in good times and bad." Msgr. Rodríguez Maradiaga always supported us in this fight.

When Alejandro was appointed ambassador, Maradiaga was happy, although he had nothing to do with Alejandro's appointment. During his trips to Rome he stayed in the convent of the Oblates of Divine Love, which was the residence of some Honduran nuns, but this convent was located in the San Giovanni neighborhood, quite far from the Vatican and the places Monsignor was accustomed to visit, so he frequently had to take public transportation. Since we lived very close to the Vatican, Alejandro invited him to stay in our house and he accepted immediately. Since then he never changed place; our home was his and that closeness strengthened his relationship with our family more and more.

Our friendship with Father Juan José Pineda (Juanjo) grew because he appeared to have many positive qualities; he was amiable, brilliant, helpful, spiritual and charming. He frequently visited our house where he would converse for hours on end with Alejandro on history and religious subjects. We also would go out for a drink or a walk in the streets of Rome. He used to call our daughters "my sisters." He once told my husband that his affection for him was like that of a son for his father, and if we were ever in need, he would come running to us.

One day he told us that he had been held up and his graduation money had been stolen, and my husband reimbursed the stolen money, which was not a small amount, so he wouldn't go lacking. When the time came for his graduation, he told us that some guests would be arriving from Germany and other places and that he didn't know how he would attend to them. I told him not to worry, that I would offer a dinner for him at my home so that he could invite everyone and we would celebrate together the completion of his studies. For years, Father Pineda was like another member of our family, because the affection was mutual.

"My friend the angel"

After graduating around 1994, Fr. Pineda was assigned to Guatemala where he stayed for two years and then was sent to the Philippines, where we visited him because I was invited to exhibit my paintings at the celebration of the 100th anniversary of that country's independence. Of course, almost every day we met with our great friend who was very happy there. From the Philippines he went to El Salvador where he was pastor for a year in a church in the Escalón neighborhood in San Salvador, and then he went to Honduras to be secretary to Monsignor Rodríguez Maradiaga, who was already the archbishop of Tegucigalpa.

We planned a vacation trip to Russia with our two daughters, and it occurred to Alejandro to invite Father Juanjo since he had to visit Rome at that time. Alejandro invited him with all expenses paid, and he accepted, but our youngest daughter said that if Pineda went, she would not join us on the trip. Moreover, in solidarity with her sister, Sophie declared that she would not go either. I begged them to change their mind, but it was not possible to convince them, Rocío said that she did not like Father Juanjo, that it was obvious that he was fake and tried too hard to be nice, that he did not seem to her to be natural or sincere and that she was tired of his "jokes." Ale and I thought she was totally wrong, and because we couldn't tell Father that we were withdrawing the invitation, we had to leave without our daughters. That's something that hurts me to this day.

It was not long before Archbishop Maradiaga expressed his desire for Fr. Pineda to be named Auxiliary Bishop of Tegucigalpa, strongly insisting that he be the one chosen. My husband, as ambassador, and Mrs. Enriqueta Miquisanti, a friend of Cardinal Rodríguez and a highly respected woman with much influence and an important position in the Italian Episcopal Conference, were the two people who worked the hardest to obtain the appointment.

It wasn't easy. The first obstacle to overcome was that the General of the Order of the Claretians in Manila, when asked for references about Father Pineda, declared that in Manila, "he had friendships that were rather strange." However, we all took it to be false because of our impression of Father's exemplary conduct. I admired him very much; for me he was a model priest, like an angel. What a pity that Alejandro and I didn't have the natural intuition of our daughter Rocío who could easily perceive all that falsehood in dear Juanjo. She was the one who was correct and we were taken in like a true couple of fools.

Father had entered our lives not for good, but for evil, because he took advantage of us. Only many years later did I come to understand that he had previously been as bad a person as he is now, but had concealed it. The evil angel was disguised as a good angel. In fact, in my first book of poetry, "El Pincel y el Corazón," published in 2001, there is a poem called "My friend the Angel" written for him and another written for Monsignor Rodríguez Maradiaga. The only one I don't regret writing is the one I dedicated to John Paul II.

When Alejandro's term as ambassador ended, our friend Archbishop Maradiaga spoke with the newly elected president of Honduras to ask him to keep Alejandro for another term, as he was doing a good job and was absolutely trustworthy. So we stayed four more years. After that four-year period he did the same with the new president and so on for several terms. In his last years Alejandro became the Vice-Dean and then the Dean of the Diplomatic Corps, representing the whole body of diplomats before the Holy See in formal events.

I also remember that Cardinal Pio Laghi – may he rest in peace – during one of President Carlos Flores' visits to Rome, publicly requested of Flores during a dinner that he keep Alejandro as his ambassador for a long period of time, and he replied that he would gladly recommend him to the next president. We later learned that he did. Incidentally, Alejandro visited him and brought him a collector's pen to thank him for the gesture. I cannot deny that Cardinal Maradiaga was the person whose influence brought about our long stay, but it wasn't until now that I understood why he did it, something I will presently explain.

The investiture of the cardinal

My husband had a goal in his mind: to do everything in his power so that our beloved Monsignor Rodríguez Maradiaga would become Cardinal Rodríguez Maradiaga, because he apparently had all the qualities to be one. The problem was that within the Roman Curia he had powerful enemies such as Cardinal Alfonso Lopez Trujillo and Monsignor Calderon Polo who opposed his promotion, but around 1996 Alejandro began to apply himself to the matter using all his diplomatic sense. He informed the cardinal of every step he took, and I remember that sometimes he would tell the cardinal, "I am here because of you and for you."

Alejandro had won the friendship of Monsignor Stanislao Dziwisz, who was the private secretary of the pope, today St. John Paul II, and also of Cardinal Angelo Sodano, Secretary of State, and so they aided his cause, and finally the investiture was achieved in 2001: Cardinal Óscar Andrés Rodríguez Maradiaga, the first cardinal of Honduras, an event! True, he knew perfectly well the work of his friend Ambassador Valladares was doing on his behalf, because he was always informed of every step and every achievement in the process and apparently it made him very "grateful." He knows very well that the idea was neither that of John Paul II nor Cardinal Sodano. It was his friend Alejandro's.

Bishop Pineda's fight with "Erick"

Several years passed before Father Pineda finally became Monsignor Pineda, Auxiliary Bishop of Tegucigalpa, in 2005. Enriqueta Miquisanti arrived at the ceremony with her three daughters and two sons-in-law, and of course Alejandro and myself were present as well.

Only two years later, in 2007, an intense scandal occurred in Tegucigalpa: a priest named José de Jesús Mora, a man entirely trusted by Cardinal Maradiaga, to whom the cardinal had given the administration of the media of the Archdiocese, wrote a letter addressed to Maradiaga. In that letter he denounced horrible things he had witnessed in Villa Iris, the residence of the cardinal, where Monsignor Pineda and Father Mora also lived, as well as a man named Erick Cravioto Farjado.

Erick was a youth that Monsignor Pineda literally brought from Mexico and installed there, in Villa Iris, where a special room was given to him very close to Juanjo's room and that of the cardinal himself. The diocese bought a new vehicle exclusively for the personal use of Erick, who accompanied Bishop Pineda on his frequent trips inside and outside the country; they never separated and began to arouse suspicion.

There is a famous saying in Honduras that is very wise and should be put into practice: "If the kid is honest, let him show it." Father Mora in the letter accused Bishop Pineda of maintaining an indecorous and scandalous life while living with Erick, and linked him to two other youths whose names he provided. This letter was disseminated on the internet and the Protestants made thousands of copies to be distributed, according to the cardinal himself in a conversation with me at the time.

Although we heard about the accusations and the letter, my husband and I did not believe them. Like most who knew Bishop Pineda, we naively believed he was incapable of such behavior. We did not see a copy of the letter until several years later, around 2011, when it was given to us by the cardinal's sister and close friend of mine, Hortensia Rodríguez de Mendoza, who had begun to suspect that its contents were true, and was worried that Pineda's behavior would do harm to her brother. She, like us, did not yet suspect that Cardinal Maradiaga was actually cooperating in the scandal and helping to cover it up.

I remember that Alejandro and I happened to be in Tegucigalpa when this scandal happened, we were totally indignant and hurt by what we considered at the time to be a slander against our friend. Alejandro paid a supportive visit to Bishop

Pineda, who said he felt destroyed, but did not defend himself, even privately in his conversation with Alejandro. The cardinal did not defend him either. Alejandro contacted the Rector of the Catholic University, Don Elio Alvarenga, to propose that the University defend him, but he did not regard it as possible. Today, according to testimonies that I have received, the same rector refers to Erick as "that faggot."

When Hortensia Rodríguez gave me the copy of the letter in 2011, she asked me to take it to Alejandro so he could turn it over to the Holy See, hoping that they would act against Pineda and prevent him from undermining Cardinal Maradiaga's work. However, Alejandro was hesitant to present it to the authorities because he believed it would do more harm to the cardinal than good. We assumed that the cardinal was seeking to remedy the problem himself, although with little success at that point.

I therefore gave it in an unofficial way to Msgr. Francisco Froján, who was in charge of affairs relating to Honduras for the Secretariat of State, stating that it was only for him to see. I know of no action having been taken as a result, but Msgr. Frojan also expressed his concern about the contents harming Maradiaga.

I now realize that my husband, Hortensia, and I were all mistaken. Cardinal Maradiaga was himself complicit in Pineda's behavior, and we should have made an official report. But none of us suspected that at the time. My husband would die believing the cardinal was innocent, but Hortensia and I lived to learn the bitter truth. Now, of the three of us only I am left to speak that truth publicly.

Father Alberto Cutié, in his book 'Dilemma,' dedicated almost a chapter to this subject where he describes the ordeal that Mora suffered in Villa Iris before he was induced by threats to retract his statements. Cutié relates that Mora told him the story himself, and that he urged Mora to leave Villa Iris. That book was not sold in Honduras, but as people like most that which is forbidden, there were plenty of people who purchased it abroad.[60]

At no time did the cardinal make any decision to correct the aberrant behavior that was occurring in his own residence and Erick Cravioto continued to live peacefully in Villa Iris with his protection and acceptance. There were many who, when they visited that house, were attended directly by Erick wearing a kitchen apron and serving drinks on a tray.

Before the letter was made public, I recall that I saw something unusual on television. Bishop Pineda had moved to the city of San Pedro Sula, in northern Honduras, accompanied by the rector Don Elio Alvarenga. They went there because Father Mora was present in that city and all three appeared together on a television program. The bishop asked Father Mora for forgiveness, but he did not give a reason for his request. I was left to wonder: what was the reason for him to ask for forgiveness?

It was unclear until a few days later, when the scandal of the letter broke. I then understood that the bishop surely had already known of the letter's existence and thought that by publicly asking Father Mora for forgiveness he could put a stop to it, but he did not succeed. However, the cardinal placed Mora in front of a pack of lawyers, who intimidated and threatened

---

[60] Cutié's references to the case involve his relating the history of an unnamed cardinal, a "Fr J." and a "Bishop P.", which matches the story of Auxiliary Bishop Pineda's residence in Villa Iris with Cardinial Maradiaga and Fr. José de Jesus Mora, as well as with Erick Cravioto, who appears to have been Bishop Pineda's boyfriend. The story also matches numerous other press accounts of the affair. See Albert Cutié, *Dilemma: A priest's struggle with faith and love* (New York: New American Library, 2011), 106-108. Cutié appears to have confirmed this interpretation, as well as the exclusion of the book from Honduran bookstores, in a series of tweets on December 29, 2013, when he stated, "For some reason they forbade the book 'Dilemma' in the bookstores of Honduras. It's sad, but true... The Church needs real and concrete reforms." In response to a reader asking why this was happening, Cutié replied, "A Honduran priest says the Cardinal Rodríguez Maradiaga prohibited it because I relate the history of Bishop Juan José Pineda." See tweets at https://twitter.com/padre alberto/status/417347748439281664.

him if he did not retract his accusation, and because he did not have specific photos (let's say in "the bed"), what he had said made him liable for slander and he was forced to apologize.

From then on, the Bishop Pineda tried to live a normal life and tried to be very pleasant; he flattered people, buttered them up, made them believe beautiful things that he told them – everything he could do to win their affection – but people saw it as false and exaggerated. It was very shocking when on the day of President Porfirio Lobo's inauguration at the National Stadium, the bishop, in public, took off his stole, which is a sacred ornament, to present it to Mrs. Rosa Elena de Lobo, wife of the new president. So he won over people by practicing servility, but when someone had ceased to be useful to him, he would cast them aside.

This happened with Enriqueta Miquisanti, who was seriously ill when Pineda arrived in Rome on the occasion of an event in the Vatican. He stayed there for nine days during which he did not deign to visit or even call Mrs. Miquisanti on the telephone. When she told me this, I told her that I was surprised that not even out of gratitude had he visited her, since she had worked so hard to get his appointment as bishop. She replied that she had never expected gratitude, but she was sure she would not do it for him again if she had a second chance, because on the day of the investiture she observed something that disappointed her so much. Four days later Enriqueta died. I was left with the regret of not having asked her what it was that disappointed her so. Alejandro and I were disillusioned little by little, and with much sadness, by our dear Father Juanjo, not because of stories or gossip, but because of the evidence against him.

I remember that one day, in spite of myself, I asked Cardinal Maradiaga a question, taking advantage of the fact that he was in our house quietly packing his suitcase to leave. "Your Eminence: Father Juanjo – was he already like that, or did he become that way?" He replied with a voice of regret: "He became that way, Marthita." To my husband in reference to the bishop, he had previously asked: "What can be done if Juanjo turns out to be a cachinflín?" – an expression he used often. (A "cach-inflín" is a very small firecracker that doesn't explode because it is of defective manufacture). Such expressions were enough for me to understand that the cardinal understood the nature of his auxiliary, but little by little he changed his way of thinking. I could tell because his answers to my questions were no longer the same.

Father Juanjo had introduced me to Erick Cravioto soon after he came from Mexico as his private secretary, making it clear to me that he had brought him because the priests were very busy and his specific job was to manage the computer system. However, in Honduras there were so many people capable of doing the work that Erick was supposed to do without the complications of coming from abroad, without the need for them to live in Villa Iris, without the need to buy them a vehicle. They could do it for a normal salary – a very good opportunity for a Honduran to obtain a good job. The bishop had been traveling a lot to Mexico for reasons related to the university, and on one of his trips he returned with Erick. Some reporters were watching him and making comments in the media because they couldn't ignore Pineda's close relationship with Erick.

Several years passed and everything remained the same, but one day, according to the employees of Hortensia, Erick and Juanjo had a terrible fight. Erick left at high speed in his vehicle and Juanjo pursued him in his. Erick didn't return home and instead went to live in an apartment with a homosexual friend, a fact that was known by many people.

One day we met for coffee with Father Carlo Magno Núñez and we touched on the subject. He had learned about it and told me it was true: Erick was in that apartment. "And what happened?" I asked, wondering how the cardinal had reacted. "Nothing, everything remained the same," he responded. Erick began to live in a house that was close to Villa Iris, and continued to work there.

A failed appointment

Around early 2015 the cardinal gave money to his auxiliary for the purpose of buying a house in Danlí, in the department of El Paraíso, so that he could live there when he was appointed bishop of that place, as Maradiaga had recommended. It is more important to be a bishop of a diocese than to be an auxiliary bishop, and perhaps that is why Pineda was anxious to take the position. Moreover, he would be less watched over by journalists there. The cardinal was visibly interested in having the nomination come out in his favor.

The process for appointing a bishop is that the apostolic nuncio proposes three candidates, the pope chooses one, usually the first on the list and that one is named. Pineda was not on the list, but the pope, if he had wanted to, could have named him "with a finger," but he did not. Finally, the appointment of the first bishop of the Diocese of El Paraíso was published: it was José Antonio Canales, a discreet priest who came to occupy the house, and Bishop Pineda had to take out all his luxurious household goods that he had already put in it. What a lesson and what a setback! They never imagined it, as both the cardinal and his assistant were accustomed to do everything as they wanted, accustomed to everything going well for them at any cost. Now something had changed. Was the Holy See finally beginning to distrust them?

Villa Iris

"Villa Iris" is the name of the house where the cardinal lives. It is so-called because that was the name of the lady who donated this beautiful residence to him many years ago, as well as a foundation which manages a prestigious bank in Honduras. She was a very wealthy lady with no descendants named Iris Ulargui. According to people who were very close to Doña Iris, it was Hortensia who introduced her to her beloved brother who ended up living in her house.

This lady was very close to the Spanish priest Vicente Pastor, long the pastor of the Miraculous Medal Church in Tegucigalpa. One day, this priest told Alejandro, very indignantly, that Doña Iris wanted to bequeath her house to the diocese of Tegucigalpa so that they could build a school for children. It is a very big house with a very large plot of land. It was offered as an inheritance to the cardinal for that purpose, but Maradiaga insisted that she should bequeath it not for a school but for the bishop's residence, that is, as his own home.

Because of his insistence, the lady finally gave in and renounced her desires, so Fr. Vincent was quite indignant. Alejandro, surely curious to know the truth, told the cardinal what Father Vincent had told him while in a conversation. The cardinal put on a bitter face and with disgust exclaimed: "What a fool!" and said nothing else. So, it was clear that Father Vincent was absolutely right, because if it had not been true, the cardinal would have denied it immediately.

The truth is that, if this honorable lady had known what was going to happen to her house, which long served as her worthy home, she would not have donated it to the Church because instead of the school she dreamed of, it became "The Crazy House," as some people call it after learning of everything that has happened there, and in reference to "La Cage aux Folles," the title of a famous French film.

He betrayed me

Bishop Pineda had recommended to us a friend of his who was moving to Rome for work-related reasons. We knew of him only very superficially, and the comments we had heard about him were not good at all, indicating that he was a bad actor and a practicing homosexual. (I want to clarify that I have nothing against those who suffer from homosexual attractions but homosexual activity certainly cannot be condoned, particularly in a Catholic.) However, Pineda recommended him to us as a wonderful person, which was odd because a few years ago he himself had told us that this friend had been expelled from a school where he was studying. Alejandro and I wanted to be polite to him, so we offered him a welcome dinner, and placed ourselves at his service. Surprisingly, two months later, we learned that he was speaking very badly about us without the slightest reason.

This individual had done something horrible to our detriment, and so when I was back in Honduras I went to Villa Iris and told Pineda, letting him know that my purpose in doing so was so that he wouldn't be deceived. However, he couldn't hide his displeasure at what I was telling him. I only told him the truth about what had happened, but it was as if I was offending him and insulting his mother.

He suddenly stood up, very upset, saying that he was going to bring me a glass of water, but it was only a pretext to get up because he could not hide his disagreement. On top of that he told me that I was offending him. Father! What did I say to make you feel offended? You couldn't answer because I only told you what had happened in a natural way and without any additional comments. I was the one who was offended because he treated me badly, as if I had invented something. That wasn't the Juanjo I knew and I left immediately. The glass of water remained untouched.

Several months later, Hortensia, who was an honorable and very good lady, told me that Pineda, in order to defend the deplorable actions of this same homosexual friend, had told her that he would place his hands in the fire for that friend, but not for Doña Marthita. That fell on me like a bucket of cold water. I couldn't believe it and I decided to ask him face to face.

I wanted to make a formal appointment and so I called his secretary who granted it to me without asking Pineda, because he knew the degree of friendship we had, and I showed up at the appointed day and time. When Father saw me waiting for him outside of his office in the chancery he did not say a word to me, nor give a smile, nor any gesture of pleasure, but he was forced to receive me. I told him what Hortensia had told me, and that she had said that if it was necessary she could confirm the story to him personally in front of both of us, but he refused to accept this offer. It was clear that it was true, that he had said it and it was clear that he had betrayed me.

I told him that if he had said that he was putting his hands in the fire for some prostitute and not for me, he would not have offended me so much, but for a guy like that, who was widely known as a very bad person, scheming, vengeful, hypocritical, capable of committing any evil, he could not be forgiven.

After that, Hortensia told me that Father Pineda had told her that when I went to visit him to tell him about the episode of his homosexual friend, I had thrown a glass of water in his face. Unbelieving, she went to Villa Iris to ask the maid what had happened to that glass of water that Fr. Pineda brought me and she said to her: "It was left there on the table. She did not drink it."

"Lies have short legs." I have related this anecdote only to show how dangerous this bishop can be, that he is capable of convincing anyone of a falsehood. Hortensia decided to investigate, because, as she told me, she didn't think I could do such a thing. However, if she hadn't known me well, she would have believed it. I later forgave Juanjo completely and the cordiality returned to our relationship, but never as before.

CHAPTER II

THEFT AND BETRAYAL

Some very important manuscripts

In early 2010 I had lent Bishop Pineda a valuable collection of antique books, as well as some manuscripts by Marco Aurelio Soto, president of Honduras for two presidential terms of office: 1876-1880 and 1881-1883. The manuscripts had belonged to my husband's father, who was a historian. They had not only a great historical value but also a great economic value. The books also are a very valuable collection, because they comprise all of the issues of the *Revista Conservadora* ("Conservative Magazine") that was published in Nicaragua many years ago, and which Alejandro's father had purchased month by month, sending them to be bound in thirty volumes of thick books. Because it is one of the few complete collections that exist, its value is very high. I had lent them to Pineda because I knew they were of great interest to him, because I knew that he was passionate about antique objects and documents, both sacred and secular, and because of the enormous trust and affection we had for him.

Almost two years after I had lent the books and documents to Pineda, when I began to lose his confidence, I asked him to return them, but he fell silent. Finally, after insisting, he returned the books to me, but not the documents. (Alejandro finally donated the entire collection of books to the cardinal and it remained in the hands of the diocese, but not in the hands of Pineda, which was what I had considered to be un-just.) I began to ask him for them, but he did not reply, I let a few months go by and I asked again. I only received silence as a response.

A few days after I had lent the bishop the books and documents, I had asked him to keep them in a safe place because they were so important, and he told me that they were being kept in a place where only he could touch them. I therefore knew that if he did not return them it was probably because he had disposed of them abusively. Eventually I raised the issue of the documents to Cardinal Maradiaga while he was in Rome, and he promised me to help me recover them, but was unable to do so surely because the bishop no longer had them in his possession. I assume that Pineda had given them to his friend, President Lobo, and then passed the bill to him, but the cardinal gave me a fairly childish explanation to save his assistant, as if to say, "He's like that, and we have to accept him that way, whether we like him or not."

I was then informed, to my horror, that Juan had betrayed Alejandro by plotting a series of intrigues and maneuvers with that same homosexual friend to remove him from his position as ambassador. This information was given to me by a priest in the chancery offices of the Archdiocese of Tegucigalpa, who also informed me that Cardinal Maradiaga knew about the situation, because he had ordered an investigation himself to determine who was pushing for Alejandro's removal. I never learned what the motive was for Bishop Pineda's behavior.

In Rome, Alejandro scolded me for lending the manuscripts to Pineda, and was deeply saddened to learn that he had been betrayed by him. Alejandro was quite hurt and in a low voice he kept repeating: "Why is Juanjo behaving like this? I have only done good to him."

My husband dies, asking "Why?"

In April 2013 Alejandro received a communication from the Ministry of Foreign Affairs informing him that his position as ambassador would end in June, and that he was being transferred to Tegucigalpa as a professor of the Diplomatic Academy. I do not know if this was the result of Pineda's intrigues with his friend, but in any case, my husband was ready to retire, and he did not accept the new position because he felt exhausted and not in very good health. His memory, which once was so very powerful, had begun to fail, and he was increasingly feeble.

When we returned to Honduras that August, we arrived at our house in a forested area outside the city. The next day, we fell asleep early because we were tired from the trip. It was three o'clock in the morning when I heard a noise that woke me up immediately. Alejandro was not with me. I looked in the bathroom and in the other bedrooms; I then walked down the hall and I saw that he had fallen down the steps to the first floor. I believe he had been seeking the bathroom in the dark and had forgotten where to go after so many years of living in Rome.

In desperation I helped him up, believing at first that the situation was not serious, despite the fact that he was bleeding through his nose and there was a strong blow to the front of his skull. I found that he was conscious and his bones weren't broken, but then I realized that it was necessary to rush him to the hospital. He was operated on twice to remove clots from his brain. He recovered a little, but after three weeks he began to suffer brain death, and after another three weeks he left on his final journey.

He didn't talk much, speaking only in very short phrases. One day I heard him say, "Why did Juanjo . . ." and nothing more. Obviously it was something that mortified him and hurt him: the betrayal of his beloved Juanjo.

I know that Alejandro had sensed his death approaching because several times he had expressed in Rome that he was returning to Honduras to die. God has his plans for us and I believe that no one dies a day before. Ale was happy; he did in
life what he liked to do, he always worked on what he loved,
and he was a winner. He had brought about the great growth of
the film company of which he was the manager for many years.
All the employees loved him and appreciated him because he
was a good and just leader. In diplomacy he reached the top,
which is to be Dean of the Diplomatic Corps before the Holy
See, one of the most important positions in the world. He received honors in life and posthumous honors as well, although
that is the least important thing. He had a happy marriage and
two wonderful daughters. His mother said he was his best of
sons and his daughters said he was the best of fathers. He lived
76 years in good health and when he was beginning to have a
neurological disorder, he left in the grace of God on the feast
day of one of his favorite saints. What more could one ask for?

While in the hospital, he always had a picture of Pope John
Paul II on his pillow because they had known each other personally and Alejandro had a deep affection and great venera-
tion for him. Following the pope's death, Alejandro visited his
tomb every day after attending daily Mass in St. Peter's Basilica. Alejandro died on October 22, the feast day of St. John Paul
II, and I am sure he came down to show him the way to the
Father's house.

There was a priest who came to the hospital to pray with the
sick. While he was with us, he told me that he was leaving because he had to celebrate Mass with Bishop Pineda in the Cathedral because it was the day of St. Michael the Archangel,
patron saint of Tegucigalpa. I asked him if he could take a note
to the bishop and he accepted.

At this point, my patience had been exhausted and I was
quite annoyed because I had lent Pineda something in good
faith, with affection and blind trust, but he had turned out to be
a shameless character who betrayed both Alejandro and me,

and did not even deign to answer me. Angry, I wrote the following: "Monsignor Juanjo, please return to Alejandro the historical documents that you stole from him." I did not get the slightest response. I then sent him the same request in an e-mail, which he also did not dignify with a response.

I then sent him a second letter in which I gave him a period of 15 days to return the documents, stating that if I did not receive them I would file a complaint against him with the Vatican for theft. To that message I received an immediate answer; he replied with a copy sent to Cardinal Maradiaga stating that he had already returned the books to me and that he didn't know why I was still asking for them. Immediately I replied with a copy to the cardinal: "Don't be a fool, Monsignor Pineda, because you don't even have one hair of a fool. I was very clear in my message where I asked you for the 'historical documents.' At no time have I mentioned the word 'books' to you. If you don't give them back to me, I will file a complaint against you."

His words were typical of the tempter, seeking at all times to distort sound arguments. It is clear that he began to involve the cardinal because he was feeling guilty and knew that later he was going to need him for his defense. It seemed that, like a capricious child, he was asking for the protection of his "daddy," and that's just what he received, because the next day I was visited in the hospital by an emissary of the cardinal: Father Carlo Magno Núñez.

Núñez told me that he was acting on behalf of the cardinal who was then abroad, in Dubai, and that cardinal had asked him to tell me to forget about the matter of documents, and that he did not like people fighting. He said that I was aware of the esteem that the cardinal had for his auxiliary, and implied that the cardinal would not allow himself to be disturbed by the issue. "But supposedly he has esteem for me as well, doesn't he?" I said to him, astonished.

The deceptiveness of Pineda

I was troubled greatly in determining the way to proceed. First, Pineda withholds the documents, imposing himself brazenly, and regarding me as not deserving an answer. Then the cardinal orders me to forget the matter so that the clever child will be happy. No sir, that doesn't work with me. I don't have sympathy for evildoers.

I was firm when I replied that I was not going to change my position: either he would return my documents to me, or I would file a complaint against him. I was very annoyed by his audacity and arrogance; I had spent two years demanding that he return things that belonged to my husband, and he hadn't answered me until I threatened him.

The next day Father notified me that Pineda was asking to speak with me in order to give me an explanation about the documents. I replied that I would not agree to do so because I knew perfectly well that any story would be invented and I was not willing to listen to lies. I reminded him that if he didn't return the documents, I would sue him.

I want to emphasize that what I couldn't accept was his attitude: always running over people, getting away with everything, betraying and lying. If he had been a good, sincere and honest friend, and had told me that he had some problem with the documents, I would have left things that way. Of course! However, I was already totally convinced that he was a very bad person and that he took advantage of others with total insolence.

Days after having spoken with Father Carlo Magno, Cardinal Maradiaga sent me an email, asking me, or rather ordering me, to forget this subject, claiming that he knew that the bishop had not stolen my documents, that he was going to defend him because he was his auxiliary, that I had hatred in my heart, that I didn't have to be self-righteous, etc.

It should be clarified that "hatred in the heart" is an expression very much used by the cardinal to describe anyone who stands in his way to denounce the truth; "hatred of my person," "hatred of the Church," and "hatred of the diocese" are his expressions. I wept for two days at the deception, at the incomprehensible and strange attitude of the cardinal. For the first time I saw him coming out of his mold. I realized how deceived I had been for so long considering him the champion of justice. I believed him to be right and impartial. I went to spend time with Hortensia to express my frustration to her and she also was shocked and indignant regarding the attitude of her brother.

I took my time and four days later I sent him an e-mail clarifying that what I felt in the face of the refusal and brazenness of his assistant was indignation and anger, which did not mean hatred, and that this matter was not about feelings, but about principles. I saw myself at that moment in the ironic role of the apprentice explaining to the teacher, a teacher who should be teaching me the principles upon which Christianity and the word of God are founded: truth and justice. I said that what I expected of him was that he should call his auxiliary to order and not openly take sides in his favor.

"Your auxiliary is indefensible and I am surprised that you defend him with regard to an act of theft," I wrote. "Years ago you supported me when I fought for my husband to be paid the benefits that were being stolen from him and that belonged to him for twenty-five years of work, but now in this case you are supporting the one who steals. What is the difference for you if both are robberies? The difference is that now it is your auxiliary?"

"If you say that you are aware that he has not stolen the documents, why doesn't he return them? You ask me to shut up, but where would the truth and justice be? I'm very sorry your Eminence, but I'm going to file the complaint. If you were to ask me to do something for you, you know I would, but I'm not willing to cover up for your auxiliary. You don't have to feel responsible for someone else's actions. Everyone is responsible for their own actions."

My husband was still hospitalized at the time and his state of health was worsening every day. Father Carlo Magno, who had been visiting him to give him communion, now gave him Extreme Unction. Alejandro was dying. It was at that time that Fr. Magno sent me an e-mail informing me that Bishop Pineda had told him that the documents had been given to Alejandro in Rome when Pineda had gone to the Synod of Bishops of Honduras, and I was in Honduras.

That outraged me so much it made me cry, because it was a big lie concocted by the bishop, who was taking advantage of a moment when Alejandro could neither speak, nor hear, nor reason, and therefore he could not deny it. I knew it was false because if it had been true, Pineda would have said so from the beginning, and I would have said it a few months ago to Cardinal Maradiaga when he wanted to help me recover the documents. Besides, Alejandro would have told me and would have shown them to me. I'm sure he would have done so. Those documents never entered our house again; if they had, we would have found them there, and we never did. Pineda invented it as a last resort, taking advantage of Alejandro's incapacity in a calculated way.

It was then that I made the decision to denounce Bishop Pineda for theft and betrayal of my husband on his deathbed. If Juanjo had not taken such a vile attitude, I might not have filed the complaint. Alejandro was his friend; he had helped him as much as he could. He had great affection for him, and at the moment of his agony, this bishop gave him the coup de grâce.

Maradiaga's protection?

Days later I arrived in Rome to visit my daughters and spoke with the secretary of His Eminence Cardinal Marc Ouellet, Prefect of the Congregation for Bishops, to whom I had addressed the complaint. I told him that as a Catholic, I did not feel good about accusing a bishop but that it was something I had to do out of sense of honor and dignity. "You have acted rightly," he told me. "Here, many people have read your accusation."

In the two-page complaint, I had asked that Pineda be required to return the documents and I had listed his lies very well according to the dates he had made them. Eight months passed without any reply; I then wrote a letter to remind them that I was still waiting. Again, there was no reply. It was quite clear to me that Cardinal Maradiaga was defending his auxiliary in the Vatican, and since he had been appointed by Pope Francis as coordinator of the Council of Cardinal Advisers[61] to study the reform of the Church, no one there would argue against him. The complaint remained in the cooler, and Cardinal Maradiaga remained with his auxiliary, happy and calm, laughing at everything.

Tired of waiting, and above all indignant because I knew what the reason for the silence was, I sent another letter to Cardinal Ouellet: "I now understand how things work, Your Eminence: Cardinal Rodríguez Maradiaga favors his assistant because he is his great friend, and you favor Rodríguez Maradiaga because he is a friend of the pope, and thus nothing is resolved, there is no justice. Is this the Holy Mother Church that our Lord Jesus Christ wants?" He gave no reply.

Surely Pope Francis named Cardinal Maradiaga as Coordinator of the Council of Cardinal Advisers out of personal gratitude more than anything, because during the conclave he was one of the cardinals who promoted the election of Bergoglio as pope. I witnessed all of that. I remember when the cardinal came back to the house following the conclave and told us how things had happened, and that it was he who had to talk to Bergoglio, who at first said that his health was not optimal, that he only had one lung, etc. However, in the end Maradiaga was

---

[61] Originally informally called the "C9," because it had nine members, it now has only six members remaining.

able to convince him. That was the cardinal's version, but now I have my doubts about the cardinal having to convince him because I believe he was already convinced.

CHAPTER III

MARADIAGA'S DECEPTION

In late 2012, a year before my husband and I left Rome, the three of us were talking to Cardinal Maradiaga in our house, and he suddenly changed the subject of the conversation to tell us that he had invested all of the funds of the Archdiocese of Tegucigalpa in a company that was operating in Honduras, and that they had given him 7% interest. However, Alejandro replied that we had never entered into investments with very high interest rates because we knew it was dangerous, and also that we didn't like having all of our money in the same place. "But this is safe, so I invested all the money of the diocese," the cardinal said. "I've already researched it!" he added with a tone of emphasis and certitude. That night, I asked Alejandro if he was in agreement with making the investment and he said, "If the cardinal says it's safe, then yes."

Maradiaga was a high prelate of the Church, a cardinal of the highest credibility, president of Caritas International and of so many other institutions and organizations, one who gave talks on finance regarding globalization and who handled such matters with great professionalism. He was an "Eminence" and in addition, our great friend. How could we doubt that of which he was so certain? We therefore expressed our interest and he gave us the contact details of the company's manager in Honduras, Ana Torres Licona, who contacted me by phone and told me that in two weeks they were going to pass through Rome because they were visiting several countries where they were making investments.

It was on that occasion that we met Mr. Youssry Henien, president of Leman Wealth Management. We signed papers authorizing the opening of an account at Commerzbank in Germany, because that was the bank where the cardinal had told us that he had invested the money through Leman Wealth Management, and we wanted ours to be invested in the very same institution so as not to distance ourselves from the safety that the cardinal had guaranteed us, and to follow to the letter the instructions he had given.

Our life savings were then transferred to open a certificate of deposit with Leman Wealth Management. One year later, we moved to Honduras and had to cancel our accounts at the Vatican Bank. I had been saving for several years to leave no debt at the time of departure. We had bought an apartment for a daughter paying more than half in cash, but we took out a loan to pay the difference. I had collected the amount in euros and I told her that we were going to cancel that debt, but she pointed out that if we were offered 7% interest in Leman Wealth Management, and we were paying our 30-year mortgage at 3%, it was better to continue paying, and she would take charge of it. I agreed and put the euros saved in Leman Wealth Management as well.

When I arrived in Honduras, my husband suffered his fall, and between hospitals and operations I had large expenses, which left me without lempiras, which is our national currency. The Italian company where we have the family's health insurance returned it to me in euros and I also invested them in Leman. Almost two months later, my husband passed away and I was paid his life insurance. Where would that money be better invested if not in Leman, where the cardinal had invested all of the money of the diocese because he had investigated it, and had verified it was safe? It is to be assumed that if a person of such importance does an investigation, it has to be a very good investigation, but according to the evidence that emerged later, he had done no investigation at all.

The offer of a fabulous gift

Around May of 2013, three months before we returned to Honduras, when the cardinal was in our apartment in Rome, he had asked me why we weren't going to stay and live there. I told him that was not possible because our house was in Honduras, that in Rome we didn't have an apartment of our own (the apartment in which we lived was leased by the government of Honduras) and that we weren't in a position to buy another one. "But I have the money," he told me.

I was very grateful, but at the same time I told him that I could not accept it because what he had was Church money and it seemed to me that it should be spent among the most needy and that was not our case. I also told him that I would feel very bad accepting so much money. He sought to convince me, telling me that "I have the foundation that Josefina (an elderly Spanish millionaire who had just died and at whose residence the cardinal stayed for many years on his journeys through Madrid) bequeathed to me, and when she gave me the documents she told me that this was for me to do good."

"In any case, Your Eminence, we cannot accept it. It's a lot of money," I responded. And I didn't accept it because I didn't want to feel I was taking advantage of our friendship; the response came out of me as something natural to say. However, I now wonder: why did the cardinal offer me that? Would it be because he knew me very well and he knew I wouldn't accept it? Did he already know that that investment wasn't safe? I have several hypotheses, but perhaps none of them are correct. The cardinal is the only one who knows what his real intentions were.

At the time I thought he made the offer out of affection for us, but now I realize that it could not be so because he later betrayed us, and those who love don't betray or hurt so badly those whom they love. I have never regretted having renounced this fabulous gift because I know that God sees it with good eyes and one day He will take it into account. "What belongs to the Church is for the poor, and what we have is the product of our work," I thought. Besides, if I had accepted it, at this moment I would not have the freedom to denounce what I am denouncing. There is no greater treasure in life than to be free, knowing that no one has you in their grip.

Years later, reading the news from the Vatican, I found that the pope addressing the bishops of the Italian Episcopal Conference on May 21, 2018 said the following: "It is very scandalous to deal with money without transparency or to manage the assets of the Church as if they were personal assets." He added that "we have the duty to manage in an exemplary way, through clear and common rules, what one day we will give account for to the master of the vineyard," and approvingly recalled a priest "who never, never invites to dinner or to lunch with the money of the diocese: he always pays from his own pocket, otherwise he does not invite."[62] At that moment I said to myself: "How good it was for me not to accept."

Leman Wealth Management disappears

In Honduras, Leman Wealth Management had ceased operations in 2014; they no longer had a branch there, and they asked me to communicate directly with Mr. Henien via email. I did so and apparently everything was going very well. A year later, in February of 2015 I traveled to Rome to visit my daughters, and while there, I wrote to Henien notifying him that I would not renew the certificate in dollars that was due and asking him to send it to my daughter Sophie's account in Rome. He didn't do it. I asked him again, and again he didn't,

[62] "Address of His Holiness Pope Francis to the General Assembly of the Italian Bishops Conference," May, 21, 2018, at: http://www.vatican.va/content/francesco/en/speeches/2018/may/documents/papa-francesco_20180521_cei.html.

so in my next message I told him that if he didn't make the transfer in two days, I would put him in the hands of a lawyer. He replied, "Let your lawyer communicate with my lawyer. I won't have any communication with you from now on." At that moment the alarm went off. My daughter Rocío began to look for information on the Internet with a friend and partner of hers, and discovered that Leman Wealth Management no longer existed. My oldest daughter, Sofía, was about to give birth. A few days later her son Alessandro was born. They say that every child born comes with a loaf of bread under his arm, but Alessandro was born in the midst of that chaos when we had lost everything.

We sought out a lawyer in Rome. When he examined the certificates of deposit, he told us that they were false, which was a good reason believe we would easily win a lawsuit against Henien. But how would we recover the money? That was the hard part. Then our lawyer began to do some research and discovered that Henien was an English citizen of Muslim origin. He hired a colleague of his in London to study the case and came to the conclusion that they could not sue him because under European law, we had to have signed a contract authorizing Henien to manage our money, and that contract did not exist. Such contracts are not used in Honduras, where one is simply given a certificate proving the deposit of a certain quantity of money in an account. The certificates we were given, it turns out, were falsified, and the bank whose name they bore did not have the money.

When I discovered the scam, the first thing I did was to try to contact Cardinal Maradiaga to let him know what was happening. I sent repeated emails to him from Rome explaining that Youssry Henien had disappeared with my family's life savings, including detailed documentation of the deposits I had made with Leman Wealth Management on his recommendation. I was hoping that he would at least offer me an explanation of what had happened and would help me in a lawsuit to recover whatever money we had both lost. However, during an entire month he never returned a single email or phone call, even when I left messages with his secretary. I eventually learned that he had been in Rome for part of that time, and had done nothing to contact us.

After a month of fruitless attempts to contact the cardinal, I returned to Honduras in the hope of finding him there. Before taking the plane, I prayed with all my heart and with the simplicity that I usually do: "My God, beloved Jesus, you know what the lawyers say, there is no way to recover the money, but I am sure that you will do something. I have no idea what you will be able to do, but I know that you will do it because you can do anything and I trust in you." Even though the tragedy was great, I felt confident; something inside me told me that everything was going to be fixed. My faith was enormous and I didn't feel so desperate. I remember my daughter Rocío said to me: "Mama . . . is it because you haven't realized the reality of what has happened that you seem so calm? We've been robbed of everything!" I don't know – maybe I was in shock.

A few days before I left Rome for Honduras, a friend contacted me to tell me that she had been swindled by Leman, and there were three other people she knew who had suffered likewise, and asked me if I wanted to join them in a lawsuit.

Maradiaga's strange response

When I returned to Honduras from Rome, the first thing I did was ask for an audience with the cardinal through the office secretary, whom I knew well. However, he didn't grant the appointment. I had to continue to call for an entire month, asking repeatedly for an appointment with him, before he granted it to me. I had never been treated by the cardinal in this way, particularly with regard to a matter that was so urgent and grave for my whole family, and I was becoming concerned.

In the meantime, I got together with the friend who had contacted me about having been swindled by Henien and had asked me to join her and two other people in a lawsuit, something my lawyer had sadly informed me was not a viable option. She confessed to me that she was very trusting when she made the investment because she was shown a picture of Henien with Cardinal Maradiaga in the Vatican saying that they were handling church money. It was clear that association of the cardinal with Henien and "Leman Wealth Management" had done harm to others as well.

Over a month after returning to Honduras, and after a total of two months of silence from the cardinal, I was finally received by him in the chancery office of the archdiocese. He did not say a word to me about whether or not he had done anything in the time that had elapsed since I had notified him of the scam two months earlier. I was the one who told him how serious the situation was. "You know we lost everything. Your Eminence, I sent you the documents." I had already informed him by email that the amount was more than 600,000 dollars – that is, all of our savings – and that additionally we were left with a debt of 120 thousand euros for an apartment used by a daughter that the Leman investment was meant to pay for.

I was struck by how unconcerned he seemed. He didn't say he was sorry, or that he was surprised, or that he didn't expect it, or that he had been taking steps to find out what had happened. His appearance was one of total calm. "That's why Fr. Carlo Magno (the vicar of the archdiocese) in the last two months hasn't received the 7,000 USD a month in interest we were receiving," he then told me, as if to say, "I'm going to get ripped off too, and they don't send me the interest anymore." Moreover, the figure of $7,000 per month, which amounts to $84,000 a year, at seven percent interest, indicated to me that the cardinal had invested the equivalent of at least $1.2 million in the venture.[63]

---

[63] It is notable that Edward Pentin, in his reporting for the *National Catholic Register*, gives the same estimate of the total investment made by Maradiaga in the "Leman" scheme: 1.2 million USD. It is also notable that the amount is a little less than that received by Bishop Pineda from the government of Honduras for Catholic charitable projects, which is still

I told him that we had sought a lawyer in Rome to sue Henien and that if he could join me in suing him, it would make the case stronger. He told me that that was not possible because his name could not be associated with it in any way, because news would certainly leak out, and it would become known in the Vatican, and they would remove him from the Council of Cardinal Advisers. "But why are they going to take you out if you're a victim?" I asked him in amazement. "Because people who have been swindled are not permitted to be part of it," he replied.

I was discouraged because I hadn't expected that answer, but at the time I still trusted him. However, I now wonder: Was he washing his hands of the whole affair? I'm sure he was, because Pope Francis never removed him from the Council. He also offered me money without being asked. When he told me this I thought about it and replied, "I'll accept it because at the moment I have nothing to pay for investigations and lawyers, but when I recover what I lost I will give it back to you." The next day he sent me a check amounting to about 17% of my losses. I have no idea of the source of the funds.

Today, I realize that he did this not only to wash his hands, but to bury me and my daughters forever, because from then on he closed the doors on us in a grotesque and inhumane manner; he never showed his face again. He shut me out me completely. He didn't want questions. He didn't want to give explanations. He just wanted peace. I felt totally betrayed, stabbed, mocked and trampled on. What did that money mean to the cardinal? Apparently little compared to the millions of dollars and euros he has in foundations he has inherited, the money he has taken from the Catholic University of Honduras, and everything else.

---

unaccounted for. See "Still No Action Taken Against Honduran Bishop Accused of Sexual Abuse," *National Catholic Register*, Apr. 27, 2018, at https://www.ncregister.com/blog/edward-pentin/still-no-action-taken-against-honduran-bishop-accused-of-sexual-abuse.

What arrangements had he made with Henien? What had happened to the money? Only he and Henien know, but I believe that the cardinal lost nothing. However, I lost all of the money we had saved with much sacrifice so that we could have a dignified retirement, and I have no pension (none is given to Honduran diplomats nor their spouses). It is a very difficult and painful situation, and it is also painful to see my daughters in debt for their homes because we had invested the money for paying off those debts in Leman Wealth Management.

A delicate topic

That day we spoke, the cardinal appeared to be relaxed and I had to tell him something quite delicate. I had already discussed this topic with his sister Hortensia. I had asked her if she agreed that I should speak about it to her brother, and she told me firmly, "Yes, Marthita, tell him, and make it clear that you are telling him because of the great affection you have for him. I'm tired of insisting and he's never listened to me."

After the preamble that I agreed to with his sister I said: "Eminence, you told Alejandro and me in Rome that a well-known lady from Tegucigalpa had commented that in Villa Iris you were not interested in fixing the problem that Father Mora had reported, because you have an 'understanding' with Erick and your auxiliary. You told us that you had asked the lady not to set foot in your house again, but now, Eminence, there are many people who think the same as that lady. I believe that this is something that you must not ignore so that you can remedy it, because the damage it is causing is being inflicted not only on your person but also on the Church." He made no comment. He didn't even flinch. Everything remained the same.

Hortensia sometimes told me that when she had a chance to speak to her brother and told him that people were very upset and were making rather ugly comments for that same reason, he responded by claiming that it was just gossip and gossip didn't bother him. The result is that, with the passing of the years, the problem grew like a snowball, and many people have been affected, especially seminarians and priests. As a result, many complaints arose and the pope decided to investigate. He was horrified by the results, according to some European newspapers.

Youssry Henien's shady past

As I mentioned previously, one of those who had been swindled in the Leman scam in Honduras told me that she had fallen for it because the representative for Leman Wealth Management had shown her a photo of the cardinal with Henien at the Vatican, telling her that they were handling Church money, and that that had inspired her confidence. After she was cheated, she went online to investigate Youssry Henien and Leman Wealth Management and found that Henien was accused of crimes and even found a lawsuit for fraud that a company in England had brought against Henien, one of his sons, and his company, Leman Wealth Management.

All of the information is there, and she gave me a copy. The lawsuit is dated September 2011 and the cardinal convinced us to make the investment at the end of 2012 by telling us that the investment was safe, that he had researched it. It is clear that he lied to us. It is there where his great irresponsibility lies, in having assured us of something that was not true. Today I do not know to what I should attribute this irresponsibility. The lack of knowledge of finance? Impossible! To a deliberate decision? Perhaps.

CHAPTER IV

SCANDAL AND COVERUP

A new apostolic nuncio

In early 2015 a new representative of the pope arrived in Tegucigalpa: His Excellency Monsignor Novatus Rugambwa from Tanzania, a true man of God. He had great charisma and was at everyone's disposal. Everyone who knew him observed that he conveyed a sense of confidence and peace; but neither Pineda nor Maradiaga could bend him because of his rectitude.

After so many years of scandal and outrage that had been unaddressed by the Vatican, everyone was waiting for a new nuncio, and it seemed that it was not possible for him to receive so many visits. I was one of the first to visit him; I informed him of the complaint against Bishop Pineda that I had presented because I had been told at the Vatican that the response would come by way of the nuncio. I learned from a priest friend that all sorts of people came to file complaints and accusations. I was even asked by a relative of Cardinal Maradiaga to take her there and I did so. The nuncio received and listened to everyone; it was his duty, as it was also his duty to inform Rome. I offered him a small lunch in my house because I know that Alejandro would have offered it to the nuncio and also because I was happy to do it because for so long we had represented our country at the Holy See. In those days the cardinal had recently undergone a foot operation and I sent him a note informing of the lunch and expressing my regret that he was not going to be able to be present due to his convalescence.

The cardinal tells me to lie

Several weeks after my initial meeting with Cardinal Maradiaga regarding the Leman fraud, we were sent a series of questions by our attorney in London, whom we had retained because of Henien's presence in Britain. I told him that we were not going to answer until I spoke to the cardinal, because the first question was how we had met Mr. Henien. I immediately called the cardinal's secretary to get an appointment, but as had happened before, I could not obtain one. I waited days, weeks and almost three months for a meeting that was never granted, and I decided to look for him elsewhere.

I, who was his great friend and hostess countless times in my own house, had to go as a beggar to see if I could meet with him at the end of Mass in a village where I knew I was going to celebrate because he was going to ordain some priests. I was able to talk to him for a few minutes, and I told him I was looking for him because there was something very important that I had to communicate to him.

He told me was acting to address the scam and that the CIA was secretly helping him but that it was so delicate that they were doing it behind the CIA's back, that they were going to propose to Henien that he invest money in Panama and that there they were going to do to him what he had done to us. "You have to pray a lot so that everything goes well," he concluded. I believe that all of that was his invention because it was illogical for the CIA to be helping him behind the back of the CIA itself. He only wanted to trick me into trusting him.

Finally, he told me that next week he would be less busy and that we could talk, so on Tuesday I called Villa Iris several times, but was always told that he was not there. On Thursday, Lina, one of the employees, told me that she had told the cardinal that I had been asking for him and that he had replied,

"But didn't you tell her how busy I am?" The tone that Lina attributed to the cardinal's response was that of annoyance. I told her that if I had called it was precisely because he told me that he would be less busy that week and that we could talk. "Then ask him if we can talk at the end of Sunday Mass in the cathedral," I added. I then called to ask her for the answer he had given and she said he had said that if I wanted to go, "then go," in a contemptuous way.

At the end of the Mass I was walking in the direction of the sacristy when I encountered a young priest who asked me where I was going. "I'm looking for the cardinal," I responded. "He's in a hurry to celebrate another Mass," he told me. I continued walking when further up I met a boy who asked me the same question and then told me that the cardinal had already gone. I continued walking nonetheless, until I had the cardinal in front of me. He had no choice but to listen to my question: "The lawyer needs to know who introduced us to Henien and since you had told me that your name could not appear in association with the suit we don't know what to do." "Say it was Paula Alvarado, BECAUSE THAT'S HOW IT WAS!" he stressed with authority. He left me petrified because that wasn't true, and he left.

In those days, I wrote a message to the Vicar of the Archdiocese, Father Carlo Magno Núñez, who was my friend and was partly in charge of the finances of the diocese. I asked him to help me get some data on the investment in Leman and after a few days he replied that he was very sorry but that his superior, that is the cardinal, had ordered him to stay out of it.

If everything had been clean and transparent, there would have been no reason to prohibit him from giving me a bit of information about it. Another thing that gives me much to think about is that Maradiaga refused to sue; he didn't even try. Are people permitted to steal millions of dollars without any effort to get them back?

The cardinal has an exceptional mind; he is not at all naive on the subject of finance. However, let us suppose that for

some strange reason he erred in inducing us to make the investment. Why turn his back on us? Why the horrible betrayal?

A radical change

What a transformation the cardinal was undergoing! It was sad
to see how a person can change so much for the worse, but I
mistakenly preferred to think that stress was making him nerv-
ous and upset. I invented reasons to try to justify it. The book
that I had presented in the conference room of the Vatican
Museums in 2013, I also presented in Honduras in 2014, in the
Archbishop's Palace of Tegucigalpa and Cardinal Maradiaga
read a short speech that he had written about the book. I think
I blushed in amazement at everything he said about the book
and about me. I'm sure I didn't deserve those compliments. He
certainly was very generous to me on that occasion. All the
change came when, because of him, we were swindled, and
knowing we weren't going to get the money back, he purposely
built a wall around himself so I couldn't have access to him.

What mysterious reason was there for such a radical change in
the behavior of the cardinal? He wouldn't even grant me an
appointment to speak to him; I had to look for him like a beggar at the end of two masses, and even then it was clear that he
did not want to talk to me. I sent him a note to tell him that the
mere two minutes we had spoken had only served to create
confusion, that we needed to speak more in depth.

He didn't answer me, so I wrote him a letter to explain that
the lawyer from Italy, who was well aware of the things that
had happened, told us that we couldn't lie to the lawyer from
London because if they questioned Paula Alvarado, she would
say that it wasn't true. I told him that it was he who had introduced us to Henien and unfortunately it was his name that we
would have to provide. I received no answer. I travelled to
Rome a few days later, from there I sent him a letter via DHL, I
told him that I perceived something strange, and if there was
something wrong, to tell me, to ask me explicitly and that he

knew that I always respond with the truth. I asked him for the money that he had offered me before to buy the small apartment and that I had not accepted from him, that I was now able to accept it because of the loss that we had had investing with Leman Wealth Management, something that we would never have done if he had not convinced us to do so.

I also mentioned to him that I had not accepted that money because our friendship with him was very special to us, that we had wanted to keep it pure, clean and disinterested. I stated that I didn't want to seem like I was taking advantage by accepting so much money from him, and that it would hurt so much if at this point he didn't appreciate that. My letter was full of sincerity, anguish and pain, but I did not get the slightest response. I verified that the letter was given to him in his own hands, but he ignored it completely.

At this point, my daughters already saw everything very clearly: our great soulmate, the one we considered our best family friend, was turning his back on us when we needed him most, and, if we were in serious trouble, it was because of him. I was reluctant to accept it; for me it was something inadmissible.

I wanted to justify his behavior at all costs, and in the eagerness to confirm that he wasn't truly betraying us, I asked his secretary, Fr. Walter Guillén, if he would allow me to send a letter for the cardinal to his email address. He accepted and I sent it to him immediately. I told the cardinal that in view of the trust we both had in his secretary, I was writing to him through Fr. Guillén, and also because I knew that his email was not secure as it was possibly controlled by a hacker in his vicinity. I was referring to Erick.

"At this moment I am in a state of shock," I wrote, "because finally I have come to understand that you, our great lifelong friend, our brother, our father, our pastor, the man in whom we have placed all our trust, and for whom Ale could even have given his life, are turning your back on us in our most difficult moments. However, on the other hand, my soul and my heart do not accept this reality. This is why I feel so conflicted."

I listed all the appointments I had asked for, all the messages I had left him, all the notes, all the letters, in response to which I had only received silence and contempt. "Don't worry," I said, "I won't bother you again. I understand that you are becoming more important and more powerful while we are little grains of sand. I feel like old shoes that no longer work for you, and you have thrown me in the garbage." I told him this not only because I felt it, but also with the hope that he would react.

Father told me that he read the note to him, that he listened to it very carefully, that he said absolutely nothing and that they continued working. I never got an answer. The cardinal was showing me that in reality he was insensitive; he was showing me all his bad manners and all of his arrogance. It would have cost him nothing to say something, or at least to ask Father Walter to tell me . . . anything!

It was evident that with his silence he wanted to hurt, to offend on purpose and with malice. But he was doing this precisely in the Year of Mercy! What kind of person is the cardinal then? That was something that bounced around in my mind. Aren't you ashamed to do what you're doing? If the cardinal wanted to wash his hands and avoid his responsibility for the scam, he could have told me that he was very sorry, that he couldn't help me at that moment, that he would see if later on . . . Whatever he had said to me, would have saved him from being a terrible traitor to our family. It's his unworthy behavior that condemns him, nothing more.

An excessive and perhaps unhealthy affection

I believe that if the cardinal had had no problem in helping me, if the cardinal had been able to give me some answer, anything, even just not to lose his composure, why didn't he? There had to be a reason for him to treat me so cruelly and show me so much hatred. If it wasn't for the scam, what other reason could he have?

I began to connect the dots. I thought it was possibly because of his auxiliary, because of that excessive affection that could be described as unhealthy that he feels for him, and that I had denounced his misbehavior. It is public knowledge that what he did to me he has done to other people; nobody can touch his assistant with the petal of a rose.

I know of a case in which a couple, an honorable couple, life-long friends of the cardinal, were removed from his friendship simply because the husband said that the government should not give Pineda money because that money did not go to the poor. However, Maradiaga never hinted that he would treat us the same way. While he kept my complaint dormant, the cardinal was confident and calm with me. Maybe he already felt that hatred towards me, but I believe that he concealed it and was preparing his revenge for later.

From the news I knew that there was going to be a meeting of the Council of Cardinal Advisers in Rome and that Maradiaga had to be there, and I was going to be there at that time with my daughters. I therefore had the hope that he hadn't answered my letter because he planned to call us during his stay, but he never did. Since I knew he was staying at Casa Santa Marta in the Vatican, I personally brought a note for him, in which I told him the following: "Your Eminence, as you are ignoring me, I have no choice but to ask for help at the Vatican. I am notifying you of this only out of fidelity, because for me, the very special friendship that has existed between us cannot disappear overnight, and I want to remain faithful to you."

I did not get an answer, so I felt I that had the green light to proceed, and as the saying goes, "He who warns is not a traitor." The next day I made an appointment with the Cardinal Secretary of State, His Eminence Pietro Parolin. He was a friend of Alejandro's and it was he who celebrated a solemn 40-day Mass of his death in the Pauline Chapel in the Vatican with the presence of the entire diplomatic corps.

Cardinal Parolin received me very kindly for more than an hour. I told him everything so that he could convey it to the Holy Father, since the damage suffered was caused by one of his highest collaborators, Cardinal Rodríguez Maradiaga, his great friend and right arm.

The cardinal tells me to be silent

When Cardinal Maradiaga learned that I had been received by the Cardinal Secretary of State, he sent his secretary to tell me not to go around speaking ill of him. Since I like to record everything, I preferred to answer him with a letter in which I pointed out to him that this was the second time he had told me to keep quiet, (the first had been when he was defending his assistant when I was going to denounce him). I told him that I had spoken about him in the Vatican's Secretariat of State, that I had told him of my plans to speak to them before doing so, that what I had said was strictly true, and that if he had said that what I was saying was not true, it would be he who was stating a falsehood.

"I no longer know you, Your Eminence," I wrote. "I have asked you several times to speak to me face to face, but you prefer to send me messages. You do not want to confront me because your conscience tells you that I am right, although you deny it. Your conscience tells you that you are heavily morally indebted to us, but you want to wash your hands of it. Moral responsibilities are just as important as legal responsibilities for those who live uprightly. You know that you have a great capacity to respond to us [our family] as you should, but you do not have good will. You know how much we have loved, respected and appreciated you, so you can imagine the immense pain that your strange attitude causes us, and what also surprises me is that you are doing quite the opposite of what you have preached in so many homilies that we have listened to you. When we asked for your help, you turned your back on us. You never answered any of the letters we sent you, letters full of pain, anguish, sincerity and despair. You always answered us with silence, a silence with which you offend, insult and despise. A silence absent of all justice, a silence absent of love, charity, understanding and mercy. With this silence you have betrayed 40 years of friendship, you have betrayed one of your best friends, Alejandro, the friend who was always faithful and loyal to you. You have betrayed the widow, daughters, and grandchildren of that great friend. I don't know you anymore, Your Eminence . . ."

This letter was copied to the Cardinal Secretary of State, because otherwise, Maradiaga would have torn it up and thrown it in the trash, and it would be as if he had not received it, because for him "Trash is for the trash can."

Where is his conscience?

I do not understand how a person can change so much in such a short time – and worse, a person with the title of "cardinal" who is called an "eminence," who has been consecrated to God and who is supposed to preach and act in the name of Jesus Christ our Lord! What has he done with his conscience to behave like this?

Supposedly he loved our family very much and suddenly he doesn't know us anymore. I remember his phrases: "If I come to live in Rome, you will both go to live in my apartment," he had told us some time ago. "But Hortensita would resent it, because she is your sister," we replied. "No," he replied: "When we make our vows, we renounce our family. She won't be able to claim anything from me."

Another day he told us that we were going to live in the Casina of Pius IV. I suppose he was joking, because that place inside the Vatican is unique, wonderful, a jewel. It is a small palace that was built by Pope Pius IV between the gardens of the Vatican; but according to the cardinal, he wanted the "Casina" for us; I suppose his idea was to give it to us when he was elected pope. Whether true or joking, he wanted to flatter

us. "When I retire I will go and live with you," he told us another day. "You are my family," was his usual expression. He always showed us much affection, saying things like, "This is my
Bethany," and, "Here I feel better than the king of Spain in his
palace." He used to say such things very often. I always thought
he was sincere, and always considered his presence in our
house to be a privilege and an honor, but now I am quite confused because I know that true affection can't be thrown away
just like that. I can't be angry or distant from anyone I love
because I feel devastated, and can't wait to make peace.

When we began to prepare ourselves to return to Honduras
after my husband's ambassadorship ended, I asked him if he
had any idea where he was going to stay in the future. He told
me that he had no idea at all, and thanked me with a great expression of sadness: "Nowhere am I going to find again the
support and affection that you have given me in all these years.
This has been my Bethany."

To the cardinal I only did well; I served him with gratitude
and affection. I don't think I deserved such a painful betrayal, a
betrayal that has caused so much harm to an entire family.
Only an evil person can betray someone in this way and only an
evil person can do so much harm to so many people and to an
entire diocese that is in a precarious condition, solely for the
purpose of defending, protecting and concealing one individual: his auxiliary bishop.

I already mentioned what happened to the priests who denounced Maradiaga to the nuncio: he took revenge on them.
That's why they remain frightened. That's what's wrong: the
victims of these people don't want to talk about their experiences. And they don't stop being right just because they've been
left unprotected by Pope Francis, who is instead protecting
Maradiaga.

Indignation

Several indignant friends of mine, including priests in both Honduras and Rome, advised me to turn to the media to expose everything that was happening. Almost three years had gone by without a response to my complaint against Pineda, who was mocking everyone under the protection of Maradiaga. I knew, in Rome, that the nuncio in Honduras had come to the Vatican to present many accusations that had been made against Pineda, but when they asked Cardinal Maradiaga for an account, he defended him with soul, mind and heart. The only thing left was to ask that when he died they canonize him.

There was already enough evidence to begin a trial of Pineda; I even knew that there was evidence in the Vatican that came directly to them, without going through the nunciature in Tegucigalpa. "I am beginning to prepare a defense for Juanjo," the cardinal told a relative. What defense did he prepare? He ordered priests, seminarians, professors, and employees of the Catholic University of Honduras to write letters about how wonderful the bishop was and presented them to the Vatican. I assume that it was counterproductive because it is known that the testimonies were written specifically to comply with an order of Cardinal Maradiaga.

The cardinal alleges that it is a plot against his auxiliary because they envy him. That's not true. A plot is an act carried out by a single group, but in this case the accusations and complaints come from everywhere, from many different sources, including laymen, seminarians, religious, and priests.

"Life is an indivisible whole"

One man cannot do right in one department of life whilst he is occupied in doing wrong in any other department. Life is one indivisible whole.

— *a saying popularly attributed to Mohandas Gandhi*

Why did the experience of power totally change Cardinal Rodríguez Maradiaga? I've asked myself that question several times but I also think that perhaps he didn't change, that he was already like that, but he hid it very well because it goes against all logic for a person who has a good moral foundation to act as if he had a bad foundation. The logical way to see it is that this person was not good, but he did everything possible to pretend that he was. He was deceptive. I don't deny that he did good things; of course he did and surely continues to do so. The problem is that with one hand he builds, and with the other he destroys. That isn't normal. Life is an indivisible whole.

On the Honduran Catholic channel Suyapa TV we have seen over time how they have tried to enhance his image, saying that he speaks six languages, that he has received so many awards, that he is close to the pope, that he plays the saxophone . . . they are already bored with that. He could speak 30 languages, receive thousands of awards and play 40 instruments, but if he betrays his friends, none of that is of value because he lacks a noble heart and a Christian spirit.

Drug traffickers in general are irregular in their conduct, because on the one hand they corrupt, murder and do a lot of damage, but on the other hand they help poor people in many ways. El Chapo Guzmán even had a church on one of his properties. I imagine they do this to soothe their own consciences or perhaps so that when they are caught there will be people who will speak on their behalf. I remember how much admiration the cardinal aroused when he was a monsignor, when he was not suspected of being a phony. He has been formed in his spirituality for many years, endowed with incredible energy, a brilliant intelligence and a wonderful memory, so much so, that he was made a cardinal, and so we must call him "Eminence." However, an Eminence has the obligation to be an example in values, an Eminence cannot afford to be involved in betrayal. An Eminence must be careful about what he says or remain silent; he has no right to speak irresponsibly, as he did with me and my husband.

An Eminence has an obligation to be a good shepherd and not to have discontented and divided clergy and parishioners. An Eminence does not have to remove good priests from the Church nor protect delinquent priests. An Eminence cannot become entangled in lies and has to be consistent with what he preaches. He does not have to involve himself in corruption because he has always attacked corruption. An Eminence must have the good sense to avoid suffering a fall because of naiveté or ignorance. An Eminence must be prudent and not be ridiculed for not being able to defend himself seriously against those who question him. An Eminence cannot allow himself to be swindled or involve third parties in a swindle.

I knew a lady who was offered the services of Leman Wealth Management, and sought the advice of a professional in the matter (incidentally, he is a young relative of the cardinal). He interviewed Leman Wealth Management officials to ask them questions and in the end he concluded that they were unreliable and the lady did not invest. How is it possible that "His Eminence" did not do the same by seeking advice to undertake something so serious? Why did he have to involve us without having done so? How is it possible that through such irresponsibility he lost so much money that belonged to the Church?

Is it true that he invested that money? I am constantly debating myself over this; sometimes I think he did it deliberately because I no longer see in him the person I came to know with Alejandro. It doesn't fit inside my head, that such an intelligent leader of an archdiocese and innumerable Honduran and foreign foundations, the ex-president of Caritas International, which includes at least 165 organizations from different countries in the world belonging to the Catholic Church and who manages enormous financial funds, might have fallen and taken his friends to the edge of the cliff who live in his "Bethany" and who only did him good, in contrast with Jesus Christ, who raised up his beloved friend Lazarus from the dead at the request of his sisters Mary and Martha who told him, "If you had been here our brother would not have died."

A double morality

Each person is free to do whatever he wants with his life but if a priest is unable to control his impulses, and worse if they are aberrant, he should leave the priesthood because it is immoral to be at the same time at the service of God and at the service of the devil. It's even worse to make a profit at the expense of the Church. The double morality is reprehensible from every point of view, and they must stop offending God within the Church. Enough of this hypocrisy because this double life is offensive, and has already done too much harm! Priests (except those who go along with it) are very upset and injured, and live in fear and anxiety. Many bishops do not tolerate it. We parishioners are indignant.

I know that there are serious people who for some time were warning the cardinal of the danger represented by Bishop Pineda. I also told him very subtly, of course, but he would not listen to anyone. The cardinal thought that people were convinced by the fact that he defended Pineda, but he was totally wrong because he brought about exactly the opposite effect, and people make comments about it that are very damaging to him.

Revenge and contempt

In December 2015, Cardinal Maradiaga canceled a Christmas lunch and a bonus of 25,000.00 lempiras (about 1,100 USD) customarily offered to each priest of the archdiocese of Tegucigalpa. For more than a decade, the lunch and bonus had been offered by the Catholic University of Honduras by order of the cardinal, but that year they weren't.

In January of 2016, during a meeting of the clergy, the cardinal made the following clarification: "Some of you have asked me why the traditional Christmas lunch was not given to you and you did not receive the 25,000-lempira bonus. It's simple. It's because many of you went to denounce me to the nuncio."

When I was told about this, I could hardly believe it. I thought it was rude, cruel and above all, a great injustice for the cardinal to act in this way against those poor priests who perhaps spend an entire year waiting for that little money to cover some of their needs, only because they had carried out their duty to report to the Holy See his deficient administration of the archdiocese.

As I explain below, it was all the more bitter because, as was well-known in Honduras, the cardinal had allowed his auxiliary bishop to appropriate for his personal use 30 million lempiras that the government granted him for Church projects. Those 30 million came out of the taxes of all of us Hondurans and instead of reaching the poor, they reached the pocket of a single bishop so that he could squander it on personal luxuries. Moreover, the victims who had filed complaints with the nuncio regarding Maradiaga and Pineda were later called to testify before Bishop Alcides Pedro Casaretto, and to take an oath of silence about what was said there. There are priests who, if they speak, can be excommunicated.

CHAPTER V

I GO PUBLIC WITH MY STORY

Strength from God

I thank the good Lord every day for the strength he has given me. Going through a test like this is not at all easy, but faith and absolute confidence in God have kept me serene, full of hope and smiling because from the start, I felt I had to trust fully and I have abandoned myself to Him.

One of the men I most admire for the philosophy by which he led his life is the immortal Mahatma Gandhi, to whom is popularly attributed the following statement: "The inner voice tells me to continue fighting against the whole world, even if I am alone. He tells me not to fear this world, but to move forward, carrying nothing in me but the fear of God."

One day I visited the nuncio, and as an expression of his opinion, he let me entertain very subtly the notion that perhaps the Vatican was not going to do much in my case, except to ask Maradiaga to come to an agreement with me. They had already asked that of the cardinal several months earlier and he had done nothing, and knowing him, I knew he would never do it. At the time I understood that I could not place my hopes in them, and I also understood that I had to undertake a different battle alone, a very vigorous battle, very difficult, against a very powerful and unscrupulous enemy. At that time I felt naked, vulnerable, unprotected, fragile, aware that I was alone; I no longer had my husband, my two single daughters were distant and fearful, and I had a 98-year-old mother from whom I concealed everything so as not to worry her.

That day I cried a lot, filled with a sense of impotence and great loneliness because of the situation in which fate had placed me. But I wasn't willing to allow myself to be crushed. I remember that I didn't stop crying as I drove to my house outside the city. When I arrived, I did what Alejandro always did when he came home: I kneeled down to give thanks to God because I had arrived safely.

Then I came into my bedroom, where I have all my images of saints and those that belonged to Alejandro. I knelt and my uncontainable weeping continued. I didn't say anything for a while. I started to calm down as I looked at the Virgin of Guadalupe and all the virgins I have, as well as St. Anthony, St, Joseph, St. Francis, St. Claire, St. Michael the Archangel – but above all, a beautiful Jesus resurrected with his arms open. Little by little I was feeling that I was filled with an extraordinary force. I felt as if someone had told me: Dry those tears. Put this armor on. And trust because you're not alone.

I stayed there, motionless, not saying a word, not asking for anything, and when I stood up, I was a different woman, a renewed woman. I felt as if I had been bathed in grace. I'm not used to praying the rosary; I prefer to pray spontaneously, to open my heart and talk to God, especially with Jesus. Despite being immersed in that labyrinth of pain and disappointment, my heart began to find peace and my prayer gave forth a poem which I wrote and which I pray every day:

GUIDE MY STEPS

*Take me wherever you want to take me, because I want to do
whatever you wish of me. Guide my steps, lead my walk, because I want to go anywhere you want me to go.*

*Light my long path with torches because dark and frightening
is the path; I want to see the light illuminating my fate to
achieve the peace I hope for.*

*I am carrying your heavy cross following your path, with this
weight that sometimes exhausts me, but with the strength that
you give me to bear it.*

*You are next to me, my beloved Lord. I sense it, I perceive it, I
feel it. And clearly, in the silence, I can hear your warm voice.*

*Never let me out of your hand, take me wherever you want to
take me. I'll do whatever you want because I love you. I'll go
wherever you take me.*

My poetry is as clear as pure water: I will go as far as God
wants me to go. If God wants to use me to write this book, I will
write it. If God wants this to be exposed to the light, so will it
be. I am in His hands.

The investigation

While in Rome visiting my daughters, I received a call from the
Apostolic Nuncio in Honduras, Monsignor Novatus Rugambwa, to tell me that I had to come and testify because an
investigation was being done, one ordered by the pope regarding the many accusations that had been made against Bishop
Pineda.

It was May of 2017. I appeared on the 24ᵗʰ of that month before Bishop Pedro Casaretto and his secretary, who had come from Argentina for that very purpose. The first thing they asked me to do was to take an oath before a crucifix affirming that what was said there would be kept secret, and that everything I said would be in accordance with the truth.

In my testimony, I reconfirmed the content of my complaint against Bishop Pineda. I also let them know that four years had passed without a response, to which Bishop Casareto responded, "But that's why we're here." However, almost four years have passed since then, and my complaint continues to be ignored completely.

In addition, I spoke about the problem with Cardinal Maradiaga regarding the fraud of Leman Wealth Management. They took note of it, but they made it clear to me that the case had to continue along the path in which it had begun, that is, with the Secretariat of State. After leaving the nunciature I was on my way home when I received a call from the nuncio to ask if everything was all right, since we had not seen each other or greeted each other during my visit. I told him that at that moment I had a concern and that I wanted to communicate it in writing to Monsignor Casaretto.

The next day, I returned with a note expressing the following: "I have no problem with my oath as to the veracity of my statement, but as to my oath to remain silent, this does have a limit because if my problems are not resolved, I am not willing to remain either calm, silent, or resigned because as a human being I have my dignity and I have the right to freedom of expression; therefore, I will speak." Several months went by and nothing came to be known about the investigation. All of us who had filed complaints were uneasy because no decision had been made in Rome.

The famous thirty million

I know that the Vatican has received evidence denouncing the
disappearance of 30 million lempiras (about 1.3 million USD)
that Bishop Pineda received from the government of Honduras
for charitable works – I know because I myself gave information about it to the Holy See, and I know of others who also
did so.

The history of the affair is as follows: Cardinal Maradiaga
was kept at a distance from the government of President
Porfirio Lobo, because of the constitutional crisis of 2009 that
occurred before Lobo's inauguration, in which they had accused the cardinal of being a "traitor" – a situation that Pineda
exploited to involve himself, strengthen his position with the
government, and generally take advantage of the crisis. That
how Pineda he managed to get his brother Carlos appointed to
an important position in the government, and induced them to
appoint his friends to important positions.

Bishop Pineda presented the president with a very nice project on behalf of the Episcopal Conference to strengthen aid to
Catholic schools, medical offices, orphanages, nursing homes,
etc.[64] The project was approved with a grant of more than 60
million lempiras and he was given half of the money, 30.8 million (1.3 million USD), that he received in a personal capacity.
Some time passed and the government of President Juan Or-
lando Hernández came into power. Pineda came forward to

---

[64] The document containing the grant was published by Confidencial
Honduras, and includes a list of causes that should be aided by the money, including "houses for the care of those with HIV/AIDS, formation of
youth in voluntary service to society, schools of maternity and formation
of youth regarding responsibility for pregnancy, aid to primary and sec-
ondary schools, medical aid, aid for the elderly . . .". See photocopy of
original document included in "Exobispo capitalino jamás justificó en qué
gastó 30 millones que le dio el Tasón," Confidencial Honduras, Oct. 29,
2018, at https://confidencialhn.com/exobispo-capitalino-jamas-justifico-
en-que-gasto-30-millones-que-le-dio-el-tason/.

claim the remaining 30 million without showing how he had spent the 30 million previously received. Probably for that reason, the remaining 30 million was never given to him. All this is in the public domain and has been questioned very much.[65] One of the many questions is: Why did the cardinal allow the money to be handled only by Pineda and not by the Episcopal Conference? Witnesses have reported all of this to the Holy See because Maradiaga and Pineda have never been able to show any invoice that could indicate how the money was spent.[66]

Arrogance and bad manners

Why does the cardinal trample on others to protect and defend his auxiliary and to grant him all his whims? Why does he insist on covering up his faults, removing him from all his entanglements, and hiding his double life? One of the phrases that the cardinal would sometimes say when a Honduran president or an official said something he didn't like was this: "They only last four years in power. I will always be here." But what I could never understand was that when, for example, I shared some injustice I had received from someone, he always ended up telling me this: "Remember Marthita, that trash goes in the trash can," as if to say, whoever is not worthwhile as a person has to go to the garbage. I listened to it, but it was a phrase I couldn't assimilate, even more so coming from the mouth of a cardinal. Finally, he ended up putting me in the trash can.

[65] See, for example, "Still No Action Taken Against Honduran Bishop Accused of Sexual Abuse," *National Catholic Register,* April 27, 2018, at https://www.ncregister.com/blog/edward-pentin/still-no-action-taken-against-honduran-bishop-accused-of-sexual-abuse.

[66] Over two years after the explosion of the scandal regarding the unknown use of the money received by Maradiaga from the University of Honduras and Pineda from the Honduran government to be given to the poor, no accounting of the use of the funds has ever been given. See, again, "Exobispo capitalino jamás justificó en qué gastó 30 millones que le dio el Tasón," *op. cit.*

One day the nuncio invited all of the Honduran bishops to lunch after a meeting of the episcopal conference. All bishops attended except Pineda and Cardinal Maradiaga, and the worst part of it was that they did not apologize for their absence. Their motive for doing this must have been because the nuncio was listening to all the people who were complaining. It is his duty to do so, and the only ones who fear such processes are those who feel guilty for hiding something.

My meeting with Pope Francis

A few months later, I decided to travel to Rome. I had requested an audience with the pope and with Cardinal Pietro Parolin in advance. I was received by Pope Francis on November 21, 2017. I told him that I had come from Honduras especially to talk to him. He immediately told me that he had read my letters and that he was aware of everything, adding that he had already instructed the Secretariat of State to fix my problem and to count on all his goodwill. I confess that during that small interview with the pope I felt very bad physically in spite of his optimistic statements. Perhaps it was the tension that I had accumulated and repressed for so long that appeared at that moment. I felt like I could have a stroke. I felt that when I spoke I could barely control the movement of my mouth. I felt horrible.

The next day I wrote a note to Cardinal Pietro Parolin in which I transcribed the statements made to me by the pope, but three long months went by without the slightest response. In the meantime, a good family friend, a powerful Italian businessman, offered to help me. He told me that he knew Cardinal Parolin very well and that he could talk to him to find out what was going on, and he travelled from Parma to Rome especially to make the visit. Cardinal Parolin was very well disposed, but he told my friend that the matter was no longer in his hands since the pope had told him that he was going to take care of it personally.

The interview I didn't want to give

A few weeks after my meeting with Pope Francis, I received a phone call from an Italian journalist named Emiliano Fittipaldi. He told me that he had seen references to me as one of the 50 people called to testify in the investigation ordered by the pope, and that he knew there was a problem with a scam in which Cardinal Maradiaga was involved and that I was one of the victims. I told him that I preferred to stay out of it, that I preferred not to talk about it, and he respected my decision.

I immediately notified the Vatican's Secretariat of State of this fact. I let them know that at that time I had been prudent in my refusal to give statements, but that surely in the future I was going to have to speak because much time had passed and my problem remained unresolved. A few weeks later Fittipaldi's article was published in *L'Espresso*. The title in English was: "35 thousand euros a month for the Cardinal: the new scandal that shakes the Vatican."[67]

Fittipaldi's article accused Cardinal Maradiaga of having received the equivalent of 35,000 euros per month from the Catholic University of Honduras and of having invested large sums of money in the English company Leman Wealth Management. He also said that Maradiaga had involved in this fraudulent operation the former ambassador of Honduras to the Holy See who was Dean of the Diplomatic Corps, as well as his wife Martha Alegría. He closed the article by saying that when he asked me for statements, I had said "No comment."

When it was published on the website, the headline of the article was changed to make it more attractive: "Widow Attacks Cardinal Maradiaga." That headline was very badly composed and I complained because the truth is that I did not attack the cardinal in any way; to the contrary, I did not grant the inter-

[67] Published Dec. 26, 2017, at https://espresso.repubblica.it/inchieste/2017/12/21/news/35-thousand-euros-a-month-for-the-cardinal-the-new-scandal-that-shakes-the-vatican-1.316341.

view! I had only recounted what had happened to the apostolic visitors who conducted the investigation in Honduras by order of the pope, and this journalist, who is a diligent investigative reporter, somehow learned about it and contacted me. Fittipaldi told me that he had nothing to do with changing the title; it had been done by those who run the website.

Maradiaga's absurd clarifications

The cardinal responded to the accusations very angrily and arrogantly, and of course, denied everything, claiming that he did not receive millions for personal use and that the transfers were justified by how he had spent the money. On the other hand, he claimed that money from the Church had not been invested in Leman Wealth Management, and that in any case, the Economic Council of the Diocese would have done it, not he, and he did not even know if that financial institution existed in London.[68]

Maradiaga called Fittipaldi's article a "calumny" and called Fittipaldi, "an unethical reporter, condemned to fail, who earns money with infamous books. The articles by the weekly (*L'Espresso*) are an attack on the Holy Father launched by those who are against the reform of the curia."

He tried to explain his reception of 35,000 euros per month from the University of Honduras by pointing out that the school is "the property of the archdiocese, and for that reason, the university gives to the diocese a certain amount of money about the same as what was mentioned, but not for the personal use of the cardinal. That money is used for seminarians and for the priests and rural parishioners that have few resources,

---

[68] Maradiaga's explanations can be found in "El lado oscuro de Maradiaga," *L'Espresso,* Feb. 5, 2018, at http://espresso.repubblica.it/ inchieste/2018/02/05/news/el-lado-oscuro-de-maradiaga-1.317878, and "Cardenal Rodríguez Maradiaga responde a acusaciones de revista italiana," *CNA,* Dec. 22, 2017, at https://www.aciprensa.com /noticias/cardenal-rodriguez-maradiaga-responde-a-acusaciones-de-revista-italiana-74083.

for the maintenance of places of worship, for events held in the parishes and to help many poor people."

He made these statements in Rome but after returning to Honduras he had his representatives defend him and he also did it personally. I saw an interview on Suyapa TV, and I have to explain this very well because anyone who listens to what the cardinal said will, I am sure, be completely convinced by him, but those of us who know the truth are astonished by what he asserted.

In the first place, the interviewer began by mentioning that what was there was a "persecution of the Church" – in other words, what they always say. The cardinal said that he was in a meeting in the Vatican where he had been a speaker on the topic of "Ethics in Action" and that when he finished his talk he found out what had been published, and of course he was surprised because that was a topic that had been aired in Honduras a year ago and belonged to the past, claiming it was a slander invented by an employee who was fired because he was stealing.

He said that now the topic had been brought up again by an Italian journalist from the tabloid press who works for a publication that is dedicated to denigrating the pope, who has no ethics, who tells half-truths, who has written infamous books, and who has been sued by the Vatican. He also said that the journalist has no professional ethics and that a basic rule of a communicator is to make an effort to talk to the person before writing something.

He emphasized that it was slander and that slander should not be spread. "If you hear something against your neighbor, keep it to yourself," he said. He advised that "we must follow the word of God" and added that he is at peace because he is with Jesus, and called himself a "humble servant."

Here I demonstrate the lies

I searched the internet, Wikipedia in Italian, and other sites for references to the Italian journalist who denounced Maradiaga. What did I find? A highly respected investigative journalist, a man of great credibility for the seriousness of his writings; his books receive five stars, and corrupt Italian politicians have been brought down because of his articles. In his book "Avarice" Emiliano Fittipaldi has published secret Vatican documents and it is true that the Vatican sued him, but the cardinal did not mention that the judge acquitted him because of the "subsistence, rooted and guaranteed by divine right, of freedom expression of thought and of the press in the juridical order of the Vatican." Besides, in everything he published, there's nothing false. So, here it is very clear that the one who is telling half-truths and turning them into big lies is the cardinal himself.

I know that Fittipaldi does not write anything without having the proof in his hands, and I say this from my own experience. The day I met him personally I told him that I had read two of his books and that in the book "Lussuria" ("Lust") he had denounced Cardinal Maradiaga for having covered up for a priest named Enrique Vásquez who had fled Costa Rica after having committed crimes of pedophilia. I told him that I had read a piece of news saying that Interpol had stated that it was not true that the priest was guilty according to the investigation that allegedly had been done. (That report was later proved false when the proceedings and investigations in Costa Rica were published.) He replied: "I have in my possession the evidence of what I wrote. If I had published a lie, I assure you that Maradiaga would have sued me for millions, but he remained silent."

Secondly, as Fittipaldi is an investigative journalist and as Cardinal Maradiaga has been questioned quite thoroughly, I know that he found the report on corruption the University of

Honduras's finances in the publication Confidencial Honduras, and asked permission to use that information to write about it, and the permission was granted. Surely he made the accusation to open the pope's eyes regarding Maradiaga, because in his book "Lussuria" he had already denounced the cardinal for another reason. Why is it not true that this was done as a "campaign against the pope because they oppose the reforms of the Church"? Very simply: I had to denounce the cardinal and I have absolutely nothing against the reforms of the Church; I do not even know what those reforms are.

Those who denounced the cardinal for corruption in finances have nothing to do with the reforms of the Church. Those who denounced him before the nuncio in Honduras have nothing to do with the reforms of the Church. In short, what the interviewer said at the beginning is not true in its implication that Maradiaga is being attacked for the purpose of attacking the Church and the pope. In this case, there could be "persecution," but it would be "persecution" against Maradiaga and his nauseating behavior.

Journalist Edward Pentin gave an interview in which he says that he has contacted Cardinal Maradiaga several times asking him some questions and that he has always refused to answer.[69] Fittipaldi also mentioned in an article that he sent him a message asking if he had anything to clarify, and again, silence. So why does the cardinal complain that he was not contacted by Fittipaldi before denouncing him? The answer is simple: The cardinal knows that in Honduras few people follow the international press and that the people are ignorant about the issue, since the local Honduran press covers it up, so he seeks to deceive God's people by making them believe he is a victim. The cardinal insulted Pentin by calling him a "political hit man."

---

[69] "Cardinal Maradiaga blames 'hit man' journalist for allegations against him," *Catholic Herald,* Aug. 30, 2018 at https://catholicherald. co.uk/embattled-cardinal-maradiaga-says-he-is-the-victim-of-journalist-hit-man/.

The cardinal also falsely stated, in his interview on Suyapa TV in Honduras, that the report was a slander presented by an employee who was fired because he was stealing. It's true that an employee was fired, but that employee had 20 years of service in the management of finances and was impeccable. What happened is that he was replaced by a man named Francisco Martínez Barahona, who is a close relative of the cardinal. Moreover, Confidencial Honduras has reported – with no denial from the archdiocese – that this accusation was made by several people: lay people, priests and professors of the Catholic University.

But in Honduras, Cardinal Maradiaga has created a reputation of being an upright and blameless person and he has deceived half the country. He sued the owner of Confidencial Honduras for publishing the original report on his withdrawals of money from the University of Honduras, but because of inconsistencies the judge did not rule in Maradiaga's favor, and because Confidencial Honduras has the evidence proving the truth of their allegations. So then the cardinal went to some of his friends who are owners of La Colonia supermarket, to induce them to remove their advertising from Confidencial Honduras. They did so because they believed Maradiaga that the journalist was indeed a slanderer and that Maradiaga was his victim. "Make a good name for yourself and go to sleep," the saying goes. But there is also another saying that says: "Not everything that glitters is gold."

Another lie Maradiaga stated is the claim that *L'Espresso* is dedicated to defaming the pope and the Church. Fittipaldi himself told me that he has enough material to write many articles against Maradiaga and Pineda but that his superior does not allow it because it will seem that he has something personal against them.

One true statement the cardinal made is that "we should not spread slander," but these reports are not slander. They are truths and the truth can be disseminated. What the cardinal never imagined was that the journalist was going to publish these proofs. The proofs can be found in the same *L'Espresso* article, "35 thousand euros a month for the Cardinal," which includes 9 pages of accounting records that appear as evidence. If you compare the report given by the bishops to the pope covering the year 2016, there were 8.9 million lempiras for tithes, but the university gave 14.5 million (almost 600,000 UDS) to the cardinal alone in the same period which is neither reported nor justified in the report.[70] Where are they? What were they spent on? Only the cardinal knows.

It is true that charity work is done with the money of the University but that money is received by the diocese itself. However, apart from that, the bishops' report reflects what the cardinal was receiving personally on a monthly basis, which is one million lempiras a month (about 41,000 USD) plus an additional million and a half (about 61,000 USD) in December of each year. That report does not show what he spends it on. If it is spent on what he says, why doesn't the report show evidence of it? If that money were for diocesan expenses as he said, then logic would suggest that the check would be in the name of the diocese.

According to a document published by Confidencial Honduras in 2016, Cardinal Óscar Andrés Rodríguez Maradiaga received 130 million which to date has not been accounted for.[71] I understand that the check that for years was given to the cardinal in his name has now been issued to him in the name of "Archdiocese of Tegucigalpa," but that money is always for him personally. I have been informed by a source close to the matter, that the money that is spent for the Church is only from an account called the "Archbishop's Curia" and the checks are issued in its name. So the explanation given by the cardinal,

---

[70] This is confirmed by internal accounting documents published by L'Espresso. See, "El lado oscuro de Maradiaga," *L'Espresso*, Feb. 5, 2018, at http://espresso.repubblica.it/inchieste/2018/02/05/news/el-lado-oscuro-de-maradiaga-1.317878.

[71] See translation of article, "Corruption at Catholic University led to fall of Cardinal Rodrguez," in the appendix.

that the money he receives personally is spent to help the poor and the priests, cannot be true. Such expenditures are funded not by what he receives, but by what the curia receives.

Why does the cardinal not document with receipts and invoices what he says he spends on the poor and the priests? Why can't the cardinal defend himself by presenting proofs of this kind? I suppose it's because he doesn't have them. It is also to be assumed that the mysterious purpose for which the cardinal has used those millions might be a dark one, because otherwise he would not hide it.

What completely perplexes me is the fact that the cardinal has told this whole series of lies, trying to deceive an entire people, his faithful! How is such cynicism possible when he himself mentioned that he had just given a lecture on the subject of "Ethics in Action"? How can he say that he is at peace because he is in the hands of the Lord? Is that what it is to be in the hands of the Lord? That's simply being in the hands of Satan, isn't it?

In analyzing Cardinal Maradiaga's response we can see all of the falsehood and hypocrisy of the cardinal. Besides, it is an act of cowardice to always use Pope Francis to hide and escape from his faults. I am sure that if it were true that he is slandered as seriously as he says, what he would have done is to sue the journalist and the media for slander. But since he knows that he would lose, he prefers to attack even if he has to descend so low.

I decide to give the interview

I was so hurt and outraged to learn that the cardinal had emphatically denied his investment in Leman Wealth Management! How dare he deny such a thing when he had convinced us to invest there? To me that was offensive, very offensive. It was cynicism elevated to the maximum! As the cardinal's saying goes, that widow for him is in the trash can and there she stays, while he is powerful and says what suits him to save himself. No sir, that doesn't work with me. I made the decision to break my silence and give the interview to Fittipaldi. I was within my rights because people's dignity should not be trampled so easily.

Consequently, I made the decision to speak because it was no longer possible to remain silent. The cardinal had been trampling on my dignity for almost three years and I was unwilling to endorse a lie that directly harmed me, my daughters and my grandchildren. I traveled to Rome to give the interview. I contacted my friend the Italian businessman, and told him more or less what I was going to say. He called his friend Cardinal Parolin to explain the situation, arguing that it would be terrible if that interview came to light. Parolin was thoughtful and worried, according to my friend, who called me to tell me that I had to contact Monsignor Robert Murphy, Parolin's secretary, because he had been looking for me.

When I made contact with Murphy, he made it clear to me that it was true that he had looked for me, but that that had been on my previous trip, to give me an appointment with Cardinal Parolin. He very kindly asked me if I wanted an audience with the Holy Father and I said no, that the previous trip had been sufficient for that, but now I had come to give the interview to the journalist Emiliano Fittipaldi because I was tired of fighting without getting results, and the world at least had to know what kind of person Cardinal Maradiaga, the right arm of the pope, really was.

Cardinal Parolin tries to stop the interview

The following day at 8 a.m. my cellphone rang. It was the Secretary of State, Cardinal Pietro Parolin, who asked me if I could delay the interview for a little while, since he had spoken with the Holy Father and he wanted me to meet with Cardinal Maradiaga who would be arriving in Rome in a week. I asked him what the objective of that meeting would be, and he told me it was for the purpose of clarifying things. "But if everything is clear," I asked him, "what else should be clarified? But, well, if it is the pope who is asking for it, I accept."

I also told him that if I were forced by the circumstances I would give the interview, but if things were settled at that meeting, I would be happy not to grant it. "Well," he said, "if you say that, let's wait for the meeting." Then I contacted one of his secretaries to tell him that I was going to arrive at that meeting with one of my daughters and my lawyer, and that it was possible that another person from the Holy See could be present.

A week passed and Monsignor Murphy, Parolin's secretary, called me to tell me that Cardinal Parolin had spoken with Cardinal Maradiaga, and that he said that he had accepted the meeting "very gladly," and that he also agreed that another person from the Vatican should be present. He told me that I had to call Casa Santa Marta, the place where Maradiaga was staying, to talk to him or leave my number so that he could tell me the place and time of the meeting. So I did. He was having lunch and I left a message. Internally I said to myself: I am not convinced that he said "very gladly," but I have to leave a margin of doubt; perhaps, because he has had health problems recently and as he knows that I did not want to grant the interview to Fittipaldi, he has softened his hard and implacable heart.

However, the cardinal didn't call on any of the three days of the meetings he attended and I informed Murphy of this. This was on March 1 and the next day Maradiaga was flying back. Murphy then told me that Maradiaga said there would be no such meeting and that he was going to see me in Honduras. "No, sir. I don't accept," I told him immediately, because he had already been asked to meet with me on other occasions and he hadn't done so. "This is a trap!"

"How is it possible that this man has deceived us all?" I asked Murphy. "He has even deceived the pope! The cardinal has taken vows of obedience! But is he believed more than the pope? This is incredible! This cardinal seems like the devil!"

"But tell me, Monsignor Murphy, who rules the Vatican?" I asked. "Does God rule or does the devil rule? Where is the pope's authority? Who is Maradiaga to dare to disrespect him, to mock him? He made fun of everyone. He did it with premeditation, treachery and advantage. No wonder he said he accepted 'with pleasure.' This is how the devil works, Monsignor: he spent the three days of the meetings calmly knowing that he was not going to fulfill what he had promised and he did what he wanted, showing, as always, all his arrogance and bad manners. But I am going to tell the world who this man really is. It is completely unacceptable for him to act with such arrogance, disregarding all ethical, moral and Christian principles without caring about anything more than himself and his assistant Pineda."

Murphy very kindly told me that he was going to see what he could do and that he would call me back. He never called me back, obviously because he couldn't do anything. So the interview was published.

Interview with Emiliano Fittipaldi

My interview with *L'Espresso* was read by millions of people because it was reproduced by many European newspapers and spread by all the networks, but above all because there was a great desire to see if the journalist Emiliano Fittipaldi would or would not provide the missing proof that Maradiaga had invested money from the diocese in Leman Wealth Management. I hadn't confirmed to him if I was going to give him the interview, but I finally did when I saw myself mocked again by Maradiaga.

In Honduras people passed the article on to each other in an endless chain. Two Spanish translations were circulated, one was correct but another was created automatically by an internet translation program and had many errors that lent themselves to confusion. I didn't read those translations but I knew that it was even said that my husband had paid money to the

Vatican for the appointment of the cardinal and that is not true; those things are not handled with money as far as I understand. I was in Rome but I can imagine the uproar in Honduras and the differences of opinion among people. I imagine it was something like in football matches: some go with one team and others with another. The important thing is that I did what I had to do and I will never regret it because it was a matter of justice. Here is the correct translation from Italian into English: [72]

L'Espresso

"Deceived and betrayed, they stole everything from me. The accusations against the pope's right-hand man.

Emiliano Fittipaldi

March 2, 2018

The wife of the former head of the Vatican Diplomatic Corps speaks out. "Cardinal Oscar Maradiaga, our fraternal friend for 40 years, pushed us in 2012 to invest our money with a London financier who then disappeared into thin air. I spoke with Francis and Parolin, but the Holy See's investigation has been stopped for a year. I am destroyed by pain and shame."

"You wrote well. Cardinal Oscar Maradiaga, the right-hand man of Pope Francis, has deceived us. In 2012 he pushed me and my husband to invest a lot of money in a London investment fund. It was operated by a Muslim

---

[72] Published in Italian as, "Ingannati e traditi, mi hanno rubato tutto. Le accuse contro il braccio destro del papa," March 2, 2018, at http:/espresso.repubblica.it/inchieste/2018/03/02/news/ingannati-e-traditi-mi-hanno-rubato-tutto-le-accuse-contro-il-braccio-destro-del-papa-1.319034.

friend of his, Youssry Henien, who then disappeared into thin air along with our money. I told Pope Francis about it all, and before that I told his apostolic visitor who conducted an inquiry in Honduras. But a year has passed, and neither I nor any of the other victims have obtained justice. It's a shame. My husband and I welcomed Maradiaga into our house for 40 years, and that's how he repaid us."

Martha Alegria Reichmann shows photos of her and her daughters together with the highly-ranked cardinal. "He has betrayed us. He has destroyed us," she repeats as if she were still unable to believe what has happened to her. Everyone in the Vatican knows her. Martha is in fact the wife of the former powerful Dean of the Vatican Diplomatic Corps, Alejandro Valladares, ambassador of Honduras to the Holy See for 22 years. He was a good friend of the Secretary of State Pietro Parolin, who delivered a moving funeral eulogy for him at the end of 2013.

L'Espresso contacted Reichmann after learning that the pope had opened an inquiry into the Archdiocese of Tegucigalpa, the bishopric of Cardinal Maradiaga – not just any cardinal, but a prelate very close to Bergoglio, who became his principal adviser after his election to the Petrine throne. Coordinator of the C9, the group of nine cardinals who advise the pontiff in the management of the universal church and in the reform of the curia, in May 2017 he and his auxiliary bishop Juan Pineda were accused of serious acts by a series of Honduran witnesses, who handed over sworn depositions to Pedro Casaretto, the Argentinean bishop sent by Francis to investigate a diocese that had been the subject of many rumors for some time.

The report has been in the hands of the pontiff for almost a year now, and he has not yet made any decision regarding it. About fifty people have been heard, and the widow Valladares is among them.

"I was hesitant to be interviewed by you because I hoped until the last moment that justice would be done without causing a public scandal. Cardinal Maradiaga was my friend for 40 years. We shared good and bad experiences, but our trust in him has always been blind, and vice versa. When he returned to our house after the last conclave, he told us what had happened. He even told us that it was he who convinced Bergoglio to accept the papacy, because initially the pope said that he was not in perfect health, he was worried about having a single lung. The intimacy was absolute. He told me and my husband that we were his family. He knows well that my husband made a big effort in the Vatican in 2001 to help him become a cardinal. At the time Maradiaga certainly had many merits, but also many enemies who opposed his cardinalate."

As she explained to Casaretto almost a year ago, "I was in Tegucigalpa and the apostolic visitor called about fifty witnesses to present our complaints against Pineda. The statements were made before a crucifix and with one hand over the Bible." Reichmann confirms that the story begins in 2012, when the cardinal suggested to her and to the Dean of the Diplomatic Corps that they make an investment with a London-based company, Leman Wealth Management. "He was a guest at our house in Rome, as was always the case when he came to the Vatican from Honduras. One evening he suddenly brought up Leman. My husband and I had never heard the name of the company or the name of its owner, a certain Henien. Maradiaga assured us that this financial company was serious, and had made investments in Switzerland, Germany and other European countries. He stressed that the investment allowed high interest rates and that it was more than certain, adding that he had also invested the money of the diocese of Tegucigalpa."

When a month ago *L'Espresso* published its investigative report on the money (about 35,000 euros a month) received from the Catholic university owned by the diocese, Maradiaga not only said that the money went to the diocese, which passed it on to the most needy (in the official budget then found by the writer, however, there is no trace of the sums of the university), but he also strongly denied that the archdiocese had ever authorized "these types of investments," even denying that he knew the society of Henien. He does not accept, in short, any accusation of "fraudulent intermediation."

The widow is shaking her head. "My husband was very skeptical about the operation. He was convinced by the insistence of the cardinal, who told us that he had done the necessary checks, and that everything was clean and safe. It was Maradiaga who provided us with Mr. Henien's contact information." The two friends of the cardinal decided to try, they met the London financier and entrusted him with all their savings. The amount is specified in the documents in the possession of *L'Espresso*. After a year, however, when the ambassador had died, the widow and her daughters realized that something was wrong. There was nothing in the accounts where Henien said he had put their life savings. The financier was untraceable. It turns out that Leman Wealth Management, according to data from the London Chamber of Commerce, closed its doors in November 2012.

"We realized that we had been scammed. We investigated, and found that this financier had already ended up in similar situations in the past. I tried to contact Maradiaga, but he refused to talk to me for months and months. I went especially to the cathedral of Tegucigalpa while he was celebrating mass, and so I was able to exchange a few words with him. He told me that he, like us, was an injured party, that he had also lost the money of the diocese, but he asked me for discretion. I told him that I had already entrusted the case to an Italian law firm also based in London but that the costs of the case were very high. He offered to help us, and gave us the money to start the legal proceedings. On that same occasion, however, he ordered me never to say that he was the one who introduced us to Henien."

The ambassador's widow knows that his accusations are serious. "I saw that after your first investigation he said that there was a plot against the pope. But it's ridiculous to think that I and my daughters, friends of the cardinal since time immemorial, could lie and invent a story like that by hurting a person to whom we have given everything. The Holy Father, whom I met last November, ordered an investigation into Pineda, a man whom Maradiaga has protected for years. I was also contacted because five years ago I reported Pineda for theft; he too betrayed my husband when he was in agony and did not have the means to defend himself. I told Casaretto that my complaint had been hidden for years, and that Maradiaga – who I still considered to be a guide – had strongly insisted that I not file a complaint. It is not the first time that he has defended Pineda even when he is indefensible."

In effect, in Casaretto's report there are some very detailed and very serious complaints from priests and former seminarians about the behavior of the prelate that Maradiaga chose as his auxiliary. "His victims now live in fear, because they have denounced Pineda and see that nothing has happened. They understand that Pineda is protected by Oscar, and it seems clear to me that Maradiaga is protected by the pope."

Despite our attempts, no one in the Vatican has so far wanted to comment on either Martha's accusations or those of the other witnesses against Pineda and the cardinal. Casaretto's dossier landed first in the Congregation of Bishops, then in Francis' drawer. "I asked for an audience with the pope and was received by him on 21 November. He told me that he was aware of my entire history and that he had already given instructions to the Secretariat of State to resolve everything." Martha hopes to recover the missing money from Henien, perhaps with the intervention of the man who had put them in touch. "Three months have passed. I spoke with Parolin and his secretaries, who a few days ago proposed a meeting with Maradiaga in the Vatican to resolve the issue. I was very hopeful about it. But after a long wait the meeting was skipped. Is it possible for a cardinal to ignore the will of the pope? I've heard that he refers to me as crazy, and that I'll never be able to regain what I've lost. Maybe. But I'm tired of being made fun of, and I've decided to tell you about all the pain they caused me. I am the first victim to take this step, but I know that others will follow my example."

The widow closes her purse and gets up. We don't know if she has the necessary evidence to convince the pope of the truth of her accusations against his most faithful right arm. But she certainly doesn't seem to be either a fool or a dangerous witch belonging to some conservative faction that wants to strike at Francis' reforms. "I hope that the pope will help me. He greeted me with words of comfort, promising me that I would get justice. He told me as if he were a father full of love."

Two months later I was also contacted by journalist Edward Pentin requesting an interview for the publication for which he writes, the *National Catholic Register*.[73] The interview was

[73] "Former Honduran Ambassador's Wife Speaks of Cardinal's Alleged Role in Mismanaged Fund," *National Catholic Register,* May 22, 2018, at

published in other media including America's *Washington Post*. I also gave interviews to the Spanish news service Info-Vaticana.[74]

Pineda accused of sex abuse of seminarians

Only two days after *L'Espresso* published my interview with Emiliano Fittipaldi, Edward Pentin of the *National Catholic Register* published another revelation about Bishop Pineda that shocked the world, but sadly, did not surprise me a bit.

The headline read, "Former Seminarians Allege Grave Sexual Misconduct by Honduran Bishop Pineda." Pentin revealed that testimony had been given to the Vatican by two former seminarians in the Tegucigalpa seminary who said that Pineda had attempted to commit sex acts with them and then penalized them when they resisted. The information was given to Bishop Casaretto as part of his investigation of Pineda.

One of the seminarians told Bishop Casarreto that Pineda "attempted to have sexual relations . . . without my authorization, during the period I was in service with him. In the night he came close to me and touched my intimate parts and chest. I tried to stop him; on several occasions, I got out of bed and went out. Sometimes I went to the Blessed Sacrament to pray to ask God that that should stop happening." Bishop Pineda, "never respected what I told him, not to touch me," the ex-seminarian added.

The other seminarian said that Bishop Pineda had tried to abuse him after taking him to sleep in a room with another seminarian during a period of pastoral work. "The pastoral work was very normal until a strange situation between the

---

https://www.ncregister.com/blog/edward-pentin/diocese-recommend-investor-accused-of-taking-widows-life-savings.

[74] For example: "Habla la viuda estafada: "Maradiaga sabe todo lo que hace el obispo Pineda," InfoVaticana, June 11, 2018, at https://info vaticana.com/2018/06/11/habla-la-viuda-estafada-maradiaga-sabe-todo-lo-que-hace-el-obispo-pineda/.

bishop and [the third seminarian] began to be seen, even sleeping in the same room" the seminarian told Casaretto. "One night we worked until late the bishop invited me to sleep with them. I was expecting it to be in a separate room; however, we slept in the same room. In the night the bishop behaved in a strange way. ... When it was early morning, he tried to abuse me; he wanted to put his leg on me and his hand also. I immediately reacted and pushed him away. The next day everything was normal for him, pretending that he had done that last night while asleep."

I think that this problem continued for a long time although it could have been eliminated at the root if Cardinal Maradiaga had acted with rectitude. However, he acted completely to the contrary. As I mentioned previously, he pretended that he knew nothing about it, giving Bishop Pineda complete freedom to prostitute himself inside and outside of the seminary.

For me, it is intolerable and unacceptable for a cardinal to allow such perverted behavior among his subordinates, and I know that many others share my views. Many people claimed that Maradiaga was involved and I believed that it was necessary for the cardinal to know, and I told him, but to no avail.

A private "hermitage" for Bishop Pineda

The accusations against Pineda confirmed what so many of us in Honduras had long known or suspected about the bishop's personal life. In 2018 I learned more that further confirmed the accusations reported in the press. A source in the Catholic University of Honduras told me of his suspicions regarding the construction of a "hermitage," an isolated place that would offer spiritual retreats on an individual basis, located on the El Tabor Campus of Spirituality, in the Valley of Angels, near Tegucigalpa. The construction of the hermitage was confirmed by the rector of the university, Elio Alvarenga, in a public announcement.

It was built with a luxurious walled apartment with all the necessary security measures (elevated wall, barbed wire and electric fence), and is operated with absolute privacy, such that the campus staff itself does not know who enters or leaves the facility, nor when. This contradicts the character and tonality of the center itself, where direct contact with nature is its principal characteristic. The "hermitage," as the source knew, was given its one "debut and farewell" with the use of a single tenant, the same Rector Elio Alvarenga who opened it with a three-day individual spiritual retreat. After this single use, the facility was converted into a second house of Auxiliary Bishop Pineda, and was only visited occasionally.

Comments and speculation led many to wonder: why did Rector Elio Alvarenga, being so zealous and fanatical about the sacred, allow Pineda to seize a facility built for the spiritual service of the university community? What forces prevented Elio Alvarenga from hindering Pineda's plans? What authority did Pineda have to turn the hermitage into his second home? Was it really the intention from the beginning to build a hermitage or was it just an excuse to establish a private place for Pineda's use? We don't know, and because of the secrecy with which the case has been handled, speculations abound. In 2015 the decision was made to host the seminarians of the pre-seminary of Our Lady of Suyapa, on the campus of El Tabor, and many witnessed the number of young seminarians who came to the private facility, invited by Bishop Pineda for "spiritual direction."

Later, in 2018, Confidencial Honduras interviewed a witness who confirmed these concerns, noting that Bishop Pineda used the place for a sleepover with one of his male friends, "Oscarito." The news service also reports that he said, in their words, that "Pineda regularly brought young men who were called acolytes, who help to officiate the mass at the altar" to sleep with him in the one bed in the one room at the facility.[75]

I return to my country

A few days later I returned to Honduras, and when I said good-bye to my daughters I told them, "This story is not over, we are perhaps halfway through. God is going to answer us in his own time."

A few days later, the cardinal appeared in Tegucigalpa giving a talk at the Lenten Breakfast, an activity that is organized every year to raise funds. What brazenness! What courage! To present oneself with dirty hands trying to make nice and speaking with phrases like this: "We should not hate anyone. There are people who, because they do not share the same ideas, fight and become enemies; there are people who do not speak to each other between families; there is nothing better than dialogue . . . We must dialogue!" He also said that we should have a not "cold heart," but a generous heart.

Nobody told me about the speech; it was I who, weeks later, changing the channels on my television set, found it on the Catholic channel. I couldn't deal with such hypocrisy and turned it off. I could not continue to see something so shameful and false. I clearly saw him as a wolf in sheep's clothing and as a false prophet. I was so indignant and horrified, but the people listening to him were spellbound, not seeing beyond their noses, ignorant of what is going on in the world.

How can the cardinal behave so hypocritically? Only a few days before in Rome he had refused to have a dialogue with me requested by the pope! It is true that one has to have the cour-

---

[75] This account was later confirmed to the press by companions of Bishop Pineda. See "Obispo Juan José Pineda dilapidó dinero en amantes, autos, motos y propiedades," Confidencial Honduras, Nov. 6, 2018, at https://confidencialhn.com/obispo-juan-jose-pineda-dilapido-dinero-en-amantes-autos-motos-y-propiedades/.

age of the evil one and be shameless in order to be able to act in this way. These are the true characteristics of a false prophet.

Pope Francis defends Maradiaga

A large part of the Honduran press remained silent about the scandals that were being published in Italy and being spread throughout the world, but when the reconfirmation of Cardinal Maradiaga as archbishop of Tegucigalpa was revealed in January of 2018, it was published in style. Oh yes, as if he had been named pope! This caused great discomfort in a large part of the population because there are very many of us who already know clearly who Rodríguez Maradiaga is and how he behaves. We know the unwholesome material that constitutes his dark side.

The strange thing has been the attitude of the pope. First, he had ordered an investigation into the finances of the diocese of Tegucigalpa and both Maradiaga and his assistant Pineda came out looking very bad, but when Fittipaldi accused Maradiaga of corruption, what Francis did – according to Maradiaga in an interview on Suyapa TV – was call him on the phone and say: "It pains me to know the evil they have done to you, but don't worry about it."[76] It is not normal, nor moral, nor ethical to support a person who commits such serious faults, and even less so in a religious institution that should set an example of decency and rectitude before the world.

According to Emilio Fittipaldi writing in *L'Espresso* in December 2017, "Francesco's friend and first counselor, Oscar Maradiaga, preached pauperism but received half a million a year from a University of Honduras. Bergoglio also wanted an inquiry into millionaire investments and into the inappropriate

---

[76] This statement was quoted by the Holy See's own news agency. See, "S.E. Cardenal Rodríguez Maradiaga: el Papa me dijo 'no te preocupes,'" *Vatican News,* Dec. 26, 2017, at https://www.vaticannews.va/es/iglesia/news/2017-12/s-e--cardenal-rodriguez-maradiaga--el-papa-me-dijo--no-te-preocu.html.

behavior of Bishop Pineda, very faithful to the cardinal. And it is precisely today that the pope speaks of 'traitors and speculators in the Church.'"[77] Excuse me, Pope Francis, but it is difficult to understand you, because on the one hand you defend Rodríguez Maradiaga and on the other hand you indirectly attack what he does. The pope has also said, very angrily, "Power and money dirty the Church!" Why then does he allow Rodríguez Maradiaga to do such things?

Pope Francis has also condemned the practice of "cronyism." Pardon again, Your Holiness, with all the respect you deserve, but we don't understand; it seems to us that with Cardinal Maradiaga's reconfirmation you have done all that you have said should not be done. We cannot explain how it is possible that precisely in the midst of the scandal in which evidence of corruption and falsehood has been extracted from Maradiaga, you have reconfirmed him. To many Catholics and non-Catholics that has been like a slap in the face to decency. Are you telling us that you support corruption and the cover-ups of sexual abuse?

With the result of Pineda's investigation, it became clear to you that Maradiaga has covered up Pineda's sexual abuse for years, inside and outside the seminary. It became clear that he has maintained a Sodom of absolute depravity in his own home, and what you are doing is keeping Maradiaga as the coordinator of the Council of Cardinal Advisers! With what wisdom can he counsel you? Perhaps proposing ideas to perfect the cover-up of sexual abuse and embezzlement of Church money?

I have read Juan Suárez Falcó's book "Masonry," where he writes: "Cardinal Danneels, in 2010, tried to cover up years of sexual abuse involving his close friend and colleague Roger Vangheluwe, bishop of Bruges, Belgium. In the meeting with

---

[77] "l cardinale da 35 mila euro al mese," Dec. 21, 2017, at https://espresso.repubblica.it/inchieste/2017/12/21/news/il-cardinale-da-35mila-euro-al-mese-il-nuovo-scandalo-che-fa-tremare-il-vaticano-1.316326.

the victim, the intimidating Cardinal Danneels ordered (the victim) to remain silent about the abuse; to 'ask for forgiveness and acknowledge his own guilt.'" Danneels was caught covering up this ecclesiastical sexual abuse scandal when the victim secretly taped the conversation. However, the mighty cardinal suffered no consequences and continued to plot and conspire to elect Jorge Bergoglio as pope.

This man fears no one and is not restricted by Church doctrine, biblical teaching, or the magisterium which he swore to uphold in his episcopal vows. Despite his solemn vows, Danneels encouraged Baldwin, King of Belgium, to sign a law in favor of abortion and supported the homosexual marriage amendment in that country. In May 2003 Danneels wrote a letter to Belgian Prime Minister Guy Verhofstad congratulating him on introducing gay marriage into the country and ending discrimination against same-sex couples. However, despite all these scandals, Francis chose him as his personal representative to the Synod on the Family in 2014, when he had no right to be part of it!

The Church is all Catholics, Pope Francis, and we have the right to understand things and we don't understand any of this. It's not possible for you to continue to have receptions like the one in Chile, where they even burned churches in protest for their cover-up of pedophile priests. These are the scandals that lead to books like Emiliano Fittipaldi's "Lust"[78] being published and movies like "Spotlight," which is about the Boston Globe's exposé on the sex abuse cover-up by Cardinal Law, being shown. Both the book and the film were produced based on serious investigations, legally documented investigations, with evidence, with testimonies! Nothing there is false. What has been Maradiaga's attitude towards these two works? He said nothing when the movie "Spotlight" was not brought to Honduras, even while people speculated that it was blocked to pro-

---

[78] That is, the Italian-language book "Lussuria," written by the journalist Emiliano Fittipaldi (Milan: Feltrinelli, 2017).

tect the Church, and said that Fittipaldi writes "infamous books." Oh, my God! The pedophile priests and bishops who rape so many children are the ones who are infamous! The bishops and cardinals who protect them are the ones who are infamous! Fittipaldi's book "Lussuria" only tells the truth.

If you read "Lussuria," I can assure you that you will weep with indignation as I wept when I learned of the case of Emma, a girl raped by a priest in Australia who ended up committing suicide because she couldn't overcome the trauma, and of the terrible suffering of her parents for the humiliation and impotence before the religious authorities, who offered them money to put an end to the problem. There is a fund in the Vatican to pay damages to victims of sexual abuse: twenty thousand dollars for each child. Is that the value of a ruined life? This is a shame and an offense to God. What they should do in these reforms studied by the Council of Cardinal Advisers is to establish immediate and harsh sanctions against rapists since they are rarely judged by civil authorities. Let them pay for their depravity rather than the children who suffer severe trauma for the rest of their lives.

Cardinal Maradiaga is the one who is coordinating the Council of Cardinal Advisers. This is the cardinal is who advises the pope. This is the cardinal who is called the "right arm" of the pope. Excuse me, Pope Francis, but we are in a bad situation. Is there no sensible person with a Christian spirit to occupy such an important position?

But what happens in our Church? My denunciation against Pineda is going to be five years old and it is as if I had not presented it. Is this justice? Is this Christianity? Is this governing the Church with the spirit of God?

I was tough, clear, and direct

On April 9, 2018, I sent a letter to the cardinal, which I also sent to several priest friends, explaining why I had finally given the interview to Fittipaldi. "For several months I addressed you many times with humility, despairing and in pain, but in response I always received an absolute silence: a silence that was insulting, humiliating, and full of contempt, an attitude unworthy of one who consecrates the bread and wine as the body and blood of Christ," I wrote. "Where are your Christian principles, Cardinal?"

Undoubtedly, the priest friends to whom I gave the letter sent it to other priests, and ultimately I think that most of the priests of the archdiocese of Tegucigalpa received the letter. It is possible that, for that reason, after several days, it reached a journalistic publication that is read worldwide, one of the few in the country and which is famous for publishing things that no one dares to publish and for not hiding anything: Confidential Honduras.

My letter was placed on their webpage[79] and they contacted me to invite me to give them an interview. The interview lasted one hour and 14 minutes.[80] It was full of sincerity and emotion without disguising my pain and anger. I was tough, clear and direct.

I begin to fear for my life

As my public profile in opposition to the cardinal began to increase, my daughters and I became increasingly concerned for my own personal safety, because of the cardinal's cynical alliance with powerful political forces in Honduras and his own personal record in attempting to silence his enemies. Honduras can be a dangerous place for those who oppose the powerful, and I began to wonder what the cardinal might be capable of. I therefore wrote a letter to the Apostolic Nuncio and to the De-

---

[79] "Óscar Rodríguez, un cardenal mentiroso e hipócrita: así lo desnuda la viuda de Valladares," Confidencial Honduras, April 25, 2018, at https://confidencialhn.com/oscar-rodriguez-un-cardenal-mentiroso-e-hipocrita-asi-lo-desnuda-la-viuda-de-valladares/.

[80] The full video can be found here: https://www.youtube.com/watch?v=dH4UCB41Tfw.

partment of Human Rights at the U.S. Embassy in Tegucigalpa. I sent a copy to Cardinal Maradiaga as well, so he would know that others had been informed regarding my concerns. Finally, I published the statement on the website Criterio.hn: [81]

"IF I AM KILLED, THOSE RESPONSIBLE ARE ÓSCAR ANDRÉS RODRÍGUEZ AND JUAN JOSÉ PINEDA."

June 3, 2018

Martha Alegria Reichmann

Editorial CRITERIO

Tegucigalpa. - Mrs. Martha Alegria Reichmann has sent a letter to the Public Prosecutor, dated May 31, 2018, in which she directly accuses Cardinal Óscar Andrés Rodríguez Maradiaga and his Auxiliary Bishop Juan José Pineda Fasquelle of being her enemies. The letter clearly states that if something unusual happens to her inside or outside of her country (kidnapping, assault, disappearance, violent assault, accident in her vehicle, another type of accident that causes her death, damage to her home, damage to her family or any other type of suspicious damage), the main suspects are the two Catholic religious mentioned above.

THE LETTER:

I am the widow of the former Ambassador of Honduras to the Holy See (1991-2013), Alejandro Valladares Lanza, and I wish to communicate the following: I have two ene-

---

[81] Published here: https://criterio.hn/si-me-matan-los-respons ables-son-oscar-andres-rodriguez-y-juan-jose-pineda-martha-alegria-reichmann/.

mies, they are Cardinal Óscar Andrés Rodríguez Maradiaga and his Auxiliary Bishop Juan José Pineda Fasquelle.

Considering that on November 27, 2013 I filed a complaint against the aforementioned bishop before the highest authorities of the Vatican, for theft of valuable historical documents and for betrayal of my late husband on his deathbed,

Considering that the aforementioned bishop acts with complete impunity, protected and unconditionally defended in all circumstances by Cardinal Óscar Andrés Rodríguez Maradiaga,

Considering: that Cardinal Óscar Andrés Rodríguez Maradiaga to whom I have never done any harm, for more than two years has treated me in the most humiliating way, as well as any person who denounces his auxiliary, without caring that in the past he told us that we were his family, because that is how we treated him during the 23 years he stayed at our house during his stays in Rome,

Considering that I have asked His Holiness Pope Francis for help in order that enormous damages caused to my person by Cardinal Óscar Andrés Rodríguez Maradiaga and his Auxiliary Juan José Pineda Fasquelle be repaired,

Considering that Cardinal Óscar Andres Rodríguez Maradiaga has shown me his hatred and resentment in its maximum expression,

Considering that for both Cardinal Rodríguez Maradiaga and his Auxiliary Juan José Pineda, I am an annoying person, for defending myself against their injustices and abuses,

Considering that my case has transcended and crossed borders, to such an extent that I am being interviewed by several European newspapers,

Considering that both Cardinal Óscar Andrés Rodríguez Maradiaga and his assistant Juan José Pineda Fasquelle have faithful friends, of terrible reputation and capable of doing whatever they tell them to do,

Considering that unfortunately in our country, Honduras, people are frequently murdered and not all cases are solved; I need to make the following clear:

If something unusual happens to me inside or outside my country, including kidnapping, attempted assault, disappearance, violent assault, accident in my vehicle, or another type of accident that causes my death, damage to my home, damage to my family or any other type of suspicious damage, I ask the following: that this notice be published immediately, and that the people listed in my complaint to the Public Prosecutor's Office be thoroughly investigated.

In the event that the crime of murder is committed against me, I kindly request of the Embassy of the United States of America that the police of that country collaborate with the Honduran police until the case is resolved and does not go unpunished as in the case of the driver of cardinal Óscar Andrés Rodríguez [Maradiaga], who was shot dead.[82]

---

[82] This is a reference to the mysterious case in which Cardinal Maradiaga's personal driver, Nelson Cárcamo, was shot and killed in his home in January 2013, by a Belgian priest who claimed to be trying to scare off a snake with the firearm. Almost a month later, the father of Cárcamo publicly accused Cardinal Maradiaga of hiding the priest, who managed to evade authorities for weeks, and of failing to contact the family to express his condolences. The priest was charged with negligent homicide and illegal possession of a firearm, but the case was halted several months

Thanking you for your attention to this letter, I place my signature below with my highest expressions of esteem and appreciation.

Martha Alegria Reichmann

Copy:

H.E.R. Monsignor Novatus Rugambwa Apostolic Nuncio.
H.E.R. Cardinal Óscar Andrés Rodríguez Maradiaga.
Department of Human Rights of the Embassy of the United States.

A meeting with the priest Bernardo Font

I received a phone call in May of 2018 from someone who told me that Father Bernardo Font Ribot wanted to contact me. I placed myself at his service and we had a meeting. He came from a small island in the south of our country called Amapala, where in recent years he had taken refuge. We met for coffee. He put a thick file in my hands so that I could read it calmly. He wanted to show solidarity with me as another victim of the cardinal. He was aware of all my history and wanted to support me publicly.

Father Bernardo Font arrived in Honduras in 1969 and was instrumental in the founding of Channel 48, the Honduran Catholic channel. He had inherited much money and property from his father, and so he also helped the cardinal financially, especially to pay for air tickets for priests and seminarians.

---

later after an undisclosed agreement was reached with Cárcamo's wife on the shooter's behalf. The case received ample coverage on Honduran television and raised much suspicion with regard to Maradiaga. See, for example: "Padre de Nelson Cárcamo, conductor del Cardenal Rodríguez, rompe el silencio," *Cholusat Sur*, Feb. 8, 2013, at http://cholusatsur.com /noticias/padre-de-nelson-carcamo-conductor-del-cardenal-rodriguez-rompe-el-silencio/.

In 2005 he was involved in a problem when he was exchanging property. A lawyer filed a complaint against him allegedly on the order of a lady named Filomena, accusing him of conducting some sort of scam. To Father's astonishment, things were finally clarified and the lady declared that at no time had she made a request to prosecute him. The lawyer was sent to prison for falsification of documents and Father Bernardo's innocence was made clear.

Surprisingly, he received a note from Auxiliary Bishop Juan José Pineda and another from Cardinal Rodríguez Maradiaga. Both with the same content: "As of this moment, you are suspended as a priest without being able to celebrate Masses or administer the sacraments." The reason given in Cardinal Maradiaga's letter was that he had "personal responsibilities with the Honduran system of justice." Confidencial Honduras has published the letter on its website. At the same time, according to Fr. Bernardo, the clergy were told that he had been suspended as a priest for having committed a crime of fraud.

Immediately his parishioners and friends withdrew from him, leaving him in absolute isolation, and consequently he fell into a terrible depression that with time became more and more acute. He spent almost ten years in the hands of psychologists and psychiatrists, taking drugs and receiving continuous treatment, and even attempted suicide. Meanwhile, the properties and businesses he had inherited from his father in Spain and Puerto Rico were left unsupervised in the hands of administrators who took advantage of him.

Finally, Bernardo recovered and resumed his life. Impoverished and aged, he wrote to the cardinal begging him to lift his undeserved and unjust punishment, but he did not answer. He wrote him a second and a third letter which the cardinal ignored completely. The corrupt lawyer had asked for Bernardo's forgiveness for having involved him in his bad deed, but the cardinal, who is supposed to love his neighbor, denied him everything as if instead of being God's representative, he was the devil's representative.

When Bernardo finished telling me his story, I asked him: "Father, what do you think was the real reason the cardinal did something so frightening to you?" "I did not like Pineda's homosexuality," he answered me firmly. He went on to tell me: "Whoever touches Pineda is trampled on by the cardinal's steel boots."

The whole history of Father Bernardo Font can be found in the online news service Confidencial Honduras. There you can read the letter where the cardinal suspends him, without following any legal procedure, without a place for defense, without a valid reason, following only his desire for revenge against those who do not like Pineda.[83] You can read the letters sent to the cardinal to suspend his punishment[84] and you can read everything involved in this case, including the lawsuit that Fr. Font filed with the cardinal for all damages received including severe moral damages, psychological damages, and long-term economic damages.[85]

"From every direction the devil is striking me"

Many people have been quite indignant to read details of my case and the case of Father Bernardo Font. This indignation has led them to express themselves verbally in solidarity with us. In my particular case, I have been approached by people I hardly know, even people I don't know at all, to give me words of encouragement: "Keep going." "Blessings." "I congratulate you on your courage." "Take care of yourself." "It was time for

[83] See "Úselo y tírelo: Cardenal expulsó a sacerdote que lo ayudó con mucho dinero," Confidencial Honduras, June 4, 2018, at https://confidencialhn.com/uselo-y-tirelo-cardenal-expulso-a-sacerdote-que-lo-ayudo-con-mucho-dinero/.

[84] See, for example, "Cura Bernardo Font acusa al cardenal Rodríguez de mentiroso y vividor," Confidencial Honduras, Sept. 17, 2018, at https://confidencialhn.com/cura-bernardo-font-acusa-al-cardenal-rodriguez-de-mentiroso-y-vividor/.

[85] See "Cura expulsado por cardenal pide indemnización de 74 millones," Confidencial Honduras, June 11, 2018, at https://confidencialhn.com/cura-expulsado-por-cardenal-pide-indemnizacion-de-74-millones/.

someone to say something." Other people have gone further and have decided to expose Cardinal Maradiaga's private statements about the matter to the press.

In September of 2018, the Spanish news service InfoVaticana published a transcript of an audio recording of Cardinal Maradiaga complaining about and discussing the cases of Fr. Font and myself in a private meeting with his priests, after year of refusing to give us any answers to our inquiries. The transcript published by InfoVaticana is as follows:

> Two years ago I received a summons from a court, in which I am being sued for twenty-two million lempiras, for unpaid wages of the priest Bernardo Font. The [legal] process had to be carried out; I also had to go to the court and declare and say it there, to show first that he is incardinated in the diocese and is not entitled to any wages or any unpaid wages. Then the guy went [to court] and the lawsuit was rejected. It is still not settled because he has appealed and it is in the hands of the Supreme Court. However, this gentleman is affiliated with a widow who has also sued me because she says that I stole her savings.
>
> That is, from every direction the devil is striking me. However, now he has the audacity to write an open letter to Pope Francis. An open letter if it is not sent closed to the addressee is also completely in vain. Well, if the recipient receives it and reads it, one can say that it is an open letter. Otherwise it is an outburst from a person unbalanced by delirium tremens and by alcoholism, who simply dedicates himself to insulting and denigrating his diocese.
>
> That man is a member of the church, he is a priest, he is a person who is mentally ill, but I am telling you so that you know, because as all kinds of garbage circulate through those networks. So that you know what this is about: this person says that I unjustly deprived him of the ministry. I did nothing more than fulfill the law of the church [regarding] delicate accusations of homosexual conduct, immediately.

He is deprived of the ministry and has no right to the ministry, because a person who has practiced what is against canon law; a priest cannot engage in business, and this is a businessman. He even has shares in Lacsa, a company in Costa Rica. They speak of him that way, but he is part of Avianca and he is a businessman. He is deprived of the ministry for that reason, but it is good for you to know because now the ducks are shooting at the shotguns, rather than the shotgun shooting the duck. And anything can happen; even a criminal can dare to denigrate his mother church. Well, [I'm telling you this] so that you know what it's all about because of all the things that these so-called social networks spread.[86]

Here I need to make something very clear. I want to show how many lies the cardinal told in those few phrases pronounced before his clergy:

1. It is not true that Father Font sued him for lost wages. He sued him for other reasons, including moral damages, abuse of authority, and the damages he has suffered from his illnesses caused by the cardinal's mistreatment.

2. The lawsuit could not continue at that moment but not because of what the cardinal said, but rather because the time to file it had expired. However, there is a law that says that if the delay was due to illness, the deadline can be extended, and that was the case of Father Bernardo.

3. It is not true that Father Bernardo and I are affiliated. We have shown solidarity, which is different.

[86] "Maradiaga se lamenta con sus curas: 'De todos lados me pega el demonio,'" InfoVatican, Sept. 13, 2018, at https://infovaticana.com/2018/09/13/maradiaga-se-lamenta-con-sus-curas-de-todos-lados-me-pega-el-demonio/.

4. When he says "a widow," naturally he's referring to me, and I've never sued him.

5. I have never said that he has stolen my savings.

6. That Father Font has written to the pope is not an outrage. It is a right.

7. Maradiaga refers to Fr. Font as unbalanced when in fact he is a healthy person who speaks truthfully.

8. He also referred to Fr. Font as an alcoholic, which is completely false.

9. He lies in the most perverse way in affirming that Fr. Font devotes himself to insulting, offending and denigrating his diocese. He has only politely demanded his rights.

10. He calls Fr. Font "mentally ill," but medical certificates categorize him as "healthy."

11. The height of the perversity was to say that there are delicate accusations of "homosexual conduct." That is slander.

12. If you say that a priest cannot engage in business, why did you accept him as a priest in the first place, given that he owned several businesses that your archdiocese benefitted from?

Those are 12 phrases that contain lies, infamies and calumnies. There is not a paragraph in which he does not especially offend or denigrate Father Bernardo, a man of God who only wants to recover his priesthood. All this has served to corroborate what the ex-nuncio Archbishop Carlo Maria Viganò said when he denounced Maradiaga saying that "he insults the victims to save himself."[87]

My decision

This perverse attitude, full of cynicism and cowardice, filled me with much indignation, and that is what sparked my definitive decision to tell this story. No, it is not possible for someone to pretend to be serving God when they are actually serving the devil. It is not possible to serve two masters at once. It is not possible to tolerate the fact that, on top of ruining people's lives, Maradiaga then denigrates them, stomps on them, crushes them in such a way that it surpasses everything that can be said with words. It was his priests themselves who, horrified and indignant, recorded and publicized these words, surely because many of them know Father Font and know that he is a good man.

I ask the cardinal: If you say that you suspended Father Font for "delicate denunciations of homosexuality," why did you never suspend Pineda with so many denunciations against him? You did the opposite, Cardinal. You spoiled Pineda, covered him up, protected him and encouraged all his depravity. Truly, Cardinal, I don't know what you are made of, and you really have a lot of talent for ingenuity and for keeping us deceived for so long.

In my letter of April 9, 2018 to you, I asked a question: "If you, in front of the international press, categorically denied that the diocese had made investments in Leman Wealth Management, and you told us that you had invested all of the money of the diocese, to whom did you lie, to the press or to us?" You remained silent. You were speechless, unable to respond. But in that talk to your priests in which you seek to justify your conduct, you told them that a widow said that you "stole her

---

[87] "Testimony by His Excellency Carlo Maria Viganò, Titular Archbishop of Ulpiana, Apostolic Nuncio," Aug. 22, 2018, at https:/online.wsj.com/media/Viganos-letter.pdf.

savings." You made that up to justify yourself, but at the moment for answering me seriously you fell silent. It is hard to imagine that an "Eminence" could act and express himself in that way. With utter irresponsibility, utter brazenness, and without the slightest shame. It would be good, Cardinal, never to forget this: "Everything you have said in the dark will be heard in the light and what you have whispered in the inner rooms will be proclaimed from the rooftops."

The deterioration of the archdiocese

If there is another reason why God will hold Rodríguez Maradiaga accountable, it is that his diocese is almost destroyed, although God endowed him with a brilliant mind to do good. There are dozens of priests who do not know what to do; it is difficult for them to make a decision because the risk is that they may end up like other priests who have been exiled without mercy. If Rodríguez did not have that incomprehensible support of the pope, it would be different.

There are fewer Catholics in Honduras every day; many leave the Church disappointed by so much hypocrisy, so much impunity and so much evil. The Catholic channel Suyapa TV and other channels are notorious for their insistence on trying to raise the profile of the cardinal, often mentioning him in the same way that politicians are promoted in the media. Vocations in the seminary have increased since the cardinal came—everything is the cardinal, the cardinal. They naively think that with that they can cover up everything.

They do not take into account, for example, that according to a study by the public opinion research firm Latinobarómetro carried out between 1995 and 2014, Honduras "presents the most emblematic case of change in religious beliefs [in Central America] in recent years." The number of Catholics in Honduras fell from 76 percent in 1996 to 47 percent in 2013.[88] Neither Guatemala nor Nicaragua nor El Salvador is equal to Honduras in such a decline. They neglect to mention that the increase in priestly "vocations" might be accounted for by the admittance of large numbers of homosexuals to the seminary.

Thoughtful young people in Honduras are no longer deceived because they know about all of this. Some elderly and poor people who do not have access to the news in the media remain ignorant and believe in the highest ecclesial authorities because they think they are faithfully representing God's principles. They are people who believe that the habit makes the monk.

The cardinal, with his skill, has been able to win over most of the owners of the main media in Honduras, who are rich, influential and powerful people. Those media have generally avoided reporting anything negative about Maradiaga and are not reproducing what is being reported abroad. They keep him well protected. They cover it up. Nor do they seem to listen to what is said about the cardinal in the few Honduran media that are courageous and impartial but that some people classify as noncredible. We all make mistakes – I was the first among those who made this one. But now I know what a great mistake I was making, because these media are the ones who do real research! These are the people who hide nothing. Nobody had thoroughly investigated the 30 million lempiras that Pineda squandered. I had to become a victim of Pineda and Maradiaga to understand this.

I remember that a few years ago on a television channel in Tegucigalpa, Channel 36, many accusations were made against Bishop Pineda and Cardinal Maradiaga. I never listened to the programs on that channel for the same reason; I was not willing to hear anything negative about Pineda and Maradiaga.

---

[88] See, "Catolicismo se redujo 29% en Honduras en 17 años," *El Heraldo*, April 28, 2014, at https://www.elheraldo.hn/pais/703487-214/catoli cismo-se-redujo-29-en-honduras-en-17-años.

Confidencial Honduras and Channel 36 caused tremendous scandals when they revealed the truth about Erick Cravioto, the 30 million lempiras and many other things. They gained a certain reputation for being unpleasant and slanderers, but we know now that they were right. They were right! Why did the victims go to these media? Simply because the others cover up for the cardinal and there our voice is worth nothing.

I am convinced that, in order to discern, we have to listen and read from various sides and have the maturity to draw our own conclusions. For my part, I have given them interviews that are broadcast in every network reaching every corner of the world. A single example is my first interview that has been downloaded 20,000 times on YouTube alone. I have also written some articles for Confidencial Honduras, Criterio.hn, and *El Libertador*. It is fortunate that they exist because otherwise it would have been difficult to denounce the evils of Maradiaga and Pineda in Honduras. That's why Maradiaga hates social networks and has called them "fecal networks," in a public homily:[89] he knows that it's useless for his friends to cover up his misdeeds if these networks are more effective in getting the word out and he can't control them as he's used to controlling everything else.

Human rights and the public prosecutor's office

At the time I had written my public letter relating my concern that I might become the target of violence due to my criticisms of Maradiaga and Pineda, I went to the Human Rights Department of some international organizations to present a similar note with several points and informing them that if something bad happened to me, the only suspects would be the cardinal and his auxiliary.

---

[89] See "Cardenal hondureño califica a las redes sociales de 'redes fecales,'" *El Nuevo Herald* Sept. 2, 2018, at https://www.elnuevoherald.com/noticias/mundo/america-latina/article217740430.html.

Later they advised me to file a complaint with the National Human Rights Commission and I did so. The Commission offered me physical protection, but I did not accept it because it required someone always to be with me. I did not accept that because I prefer to trust God fully. They also directed me to file the same complaint with the public prosecutor's office. There, too, I was very well attended to by a prosecutor who guided me on how to file the complaint. I want to clarify that I did not present this complaint to denounce Cardinal Maradiaga but to denounce the people involved in Leman Wealth Management, but I had to relate the whole history of the fraud.

After he had read my statements about the cardinal, the prosecutor told me that Maradiaga would have to be questioned to clarify certain things. The prosecutor also told me with much authority and energy: "You have to inform the pope about all this," to which I replied that he was already well aware of everything. "Well, you have to go again and insist because he has something to resolve here," he responded. I had my trip to Rome scheduled a week later but I didn't ask for an audience with the pope again; it was useless and I had already humiliated myself enough.

Later I was notified by the public prosecutor's office that my case had been transferred to the "impact unit," where special cases are resolved. Upon returning from Rome, I was received by another prosecutor from the same impact unit. He received my statement orally, a copy of which I signed, and he confirmed to me that the cardinal would have to be questioned.

I don't know if or when they will question the cardinal, but if they do, what will the cardinal say to the prosecutor? Will he be able to continue lying as he lied to the press?

Pineda resigns, unpunished

A year and a half had passed since the investigation of Bishop Pineda and not a single decision had been made at the Vatican after the dozens of denunciations against him had been confirmed. In the meantime, the press, especially the international press, was constantly busy denouncing him. If it had not been for this coverage, Pineda would surely have remained in his position as auxiliary bishop, but on July 20, 2018, the news appeared that he had resigned. That was the least expected thing: a resignation. Many of us expected a dismissal, and many, a dismissal from the priesthood, not only from his position as auxiliary bishop. However, he left as if he had resigned only because he was tired, saying that he would now have time for "prayer, meditation, [and] personal formation."

Of course, no one mentioned that there had been any fault on his part, much less any offenses. He was allowed to quietly steal a million and a half dollars from the people of Honduras and was not asked to pay for the valuable documents he stole from my family. Even worse, he appears never to have been held accountable for his sexual misconduct, and the public has never been notified of the outcome of the investigation into reports that he abused seminarians. If it had been up to the cardinal and the pope, he would never have been removed from his position. It was only because of the press allegations that the decision was made to remove him, because the scandal was already too big.

Today I can compare the case of Bishop Pineda with the case of the Honduran priest German Flores, who was dismissed from the priesthood by Pope Francis in 2019 because there were four complaints of rape against him, while against Pineda there were many accusations of every kind, but he was permitted merely to resign from his position as bishop. He continues to live his own life, and has only been moved to another place without receiving the punishment he deserves. Ironically, he has received the honorable title of "Bishop Emeritus."

CHAPTER VI

POPE FRANCIS' BETRAYAL

Why do I feel betrayed by Pope Francis?

As I have already explained in previous pages, on November 21, 2017 the pope told me that he was well aware of my case, that he had read my letters and that he had instructed the Secretariat of State to resolve my problem. He also told me that I could count on all his "good will" when he gave me his blessing by making the sign of the cross on my forehead.

Pope Francis stated to me that he had specifically asked the Secretary of State Pietro Parolin to resolve my case. However, when three long months had passed and nothing was happening, I complained to Nuncio Rugambwa and he asked Cardinal Parolin about the matter. When my friend, the Italian businessman, went to visit Parolin to ask him for an update on the case, Parolin told him that he no longer had anything to do with the matter because he had asked Pope Francis about it, and the pope had told him that he would take care of it personally. It seems that Pope Francis knew that the matter would remain unresolved and washed his hands of it. I wrote a total of five letters to the pope, and never received any response.

Why the pope's dark complicity with Maradiaga?

The pope is the pope! What can prevent him from remedying a serious fault committed by his "right hand man"? Nothing and no one can stop him. It was perfectly clear that the good will he offered me was false. Whenever I wrote to the pope I presented myself as "the widow of the Holy Gospels," that widow who went to the judge to receive justice, but he did not take care of her and time passed. However, the widow insisted so much that eventually the judge out of fatigue decided in her favor.

I told him that I expected him to do justice, more than anything as Vicar of Christ, and to remember how Jesus Christ protects widows in the Holy Gospels. The pope knows perfectly well that I have the right to ask for justice, otherwise he was free to tell me that I was not right. But no authority in the Church has ever dared to tell me that. No one.

While the pope made the sign of the cross on my forehead, I saw him as a loving father, and with those same words I concluded my interview that I gave to *L'Espresso*, but now I am sadly disappointed. I doubt that he ever had good intentions for me. It seems that the only thing that interested him was to satisfy Rodríguez Maradiaga.

In the month of October 2018, the nuncio in Honduras, Monsignor Rugambwa, was received by the pope. He had told me that he was going to talk to him about my case because it was not possible for this problem to remain unresolved after so long. As a good diplomat, he could not tell me more, but I perceived that he had great hopes. What's more, I think he was certain that the issue would finally be resolved. When the day came, he told me with much pain that he brought up the topic, but he didn't resolve anything. This can only be a product of the evil that has invaded the house of God.

It seems that in that house the teachings of Christ contained in his Biblical mandates have gone out of fashion and they want to make Francis' phrases fashionable. Where is that love of a father and of a shepherd that you tried to make me believe in, Pope Francis? It appears that you weren't being honest with me and that's not worthy of a pope. I explained, begged and humiliated myself before you as a desperate widow, Pope Francis, and what I received was what seems like only a cruel deception. I feel in my soul your hardness of heart. I would have liked you to treat me with that heart that tries to make me believe in your beautiful sayings. It is in one's actions that one follows the teachings of Christ, Pope Francis, not with your phrases that vanish into thin air.

"He that humbleth himself shall be exalted, and he that exalteth himself shall be humbled." These are words that must be taken into account because it was nothing less than Christ who pronounced them.

You are very powerful, Pope Francis. Rodríguez Maradiaga is very powerful because you allow him to be so and the two of you have united your power to pour it out against a widow. You can't imagine what it feels like. I do not believe that you fulfill the loving intentions expressed in your beautiful statements. I can affirm it because with me you have been miserly while with those who commit crimes within the Church, you have been generous, and when you have acted it was only because external pressure forced you to do so. It is not because you have a sense of justice.

I have seen a picture of you giving someone a plate of food from your "popemobile." These appear to be nothing more than acts contrived to create images to spread around the world and to make people think that you are generous, in denial of what Jesus told us: "Let your right hand not know what your left hand is doing." But you need publicity. I believed in you. I trusted you and waited for you because I thought you were representing Christ as He is: just and merciful. Instead, what you have done is disappoint me and break my heart. I'm sure God reproaches you because you are not following Christ's commandments.

Pope Francis, you don't know the psychological impact one suffers when a "Vicar of the living Christ" does that. It's scary. It's hard to put into words. I thank God that my faith is deeply rooted and I have the assurance that God will do me justice. I know that he will manage to recompense me for this injustice I have suffered. For him nothing is impossible. He *is* merciful and I only have to wait.

If I dare say these things to you, it is because you have said that the pope can be criticized. Although I am not sure that you said it sincerely. It's not that I want to criticize you; I'm just doing what my conscience tells me to do: to tell the truth, because God asks me to do so. "But all things that are reproved, are made manifest by the light; for all that is made manifest is light" (Eph. 5:13).

It seems that, as he made the sign of the cross on my forehead, the pope was lying to me. Now I ask myself, is that why at that moment with the pope I felt that strange discomfort?

The shame of the Church before the whole world

In September 2018, also in Rome, I was told by a friend that she had attended the premiere of an Italian documentary film on the sayings of Pope Francis. In words addressed to the public, the producer said that he had received a request from the Vatican to make a film highlighting those beautiful phrases that the pope recites. They are nice sayings, yes, but all this sounds to me like a campaign, like those of politicians to win sympathy. They do not seem to me to be evangelizing statements, because it is evident that they are not made with sincerity; for words to be effective, they must go hand in hand with the example of deeds, and that is not happening. I can affirm this because I have experienced it personally, and here I can demonstrate it, at least with regard to me.

The pope has said the following:

"The Church is not a tollhouse; it is the house of the Father, where there is a place for everyone, with all their problems."[90]

In that "house of the Father" I was deceived, both by Maradiaga and by Pope Francis himself.

He denounces "That 'goodism of compromises,' for the purpose of "attracting the admiration or the love of the faithful by letting them do what they want."[91]

But as a pastor, Pope Francis practices such "goodism" with Maradiaga, with McCarrick, with Danneels, with Peña Parra and with all those who have the same characteristics.

"It is not healthy to love silence while fleeing interaction with others."[92]

But confronted by Viganò's report, not being able to deny it, he changed his mind and advocated "silence," for "people lacking good will, with people who only seek scandal, who seek only division, who seek only destruction."[93]

---

[90] Apostolic exhortation *Gaudete et Exultate,* March 19, 2018, par. 47, at http://www.vatican.va/content/francesco/en/apost_exhortations/documents/papa-francesco_esortazione-ap_20180319_gaudete-et-exsultate.html.

[91] "Papa: Como Don Milani, asistamos a los demás sin buenismos," Radio Vaticano, June 22, 2017, at http://www.archivioradiovaticana.va/storico/2017/06/22/papa_como_don_milani,_asistamos_a_los_demás_sin_buenismos/es-1320626.

[92] Apostolic exhortation *Gaudete et Exultate,* par. 26, *op. cit.*

[93] "As abuse controversy swirls, Pope Francis says those who 'seek scandal' should be met with prayer and silence," Associated Press, Sept. 3, 2018, at https://nationalpost.com/news/world/popes-remedy-to-those-seeking-scandal-prayer-and-silence.

"The good shepherd knows how to denounce, using first and last names."[94]

But he allows this evil that is denounced to continue to harm victims and the Church.

"Oh, how I would like a poor Church, and for the poor."[95]

But he allows Maradiaga to have the wealth, as well as other cardinals who misuse the resources of the Church, such as Cardinal Bertone, who took funds from hospital donations to refurbish his apartment.

"These are the great idols: success, power and money. They are timeless temptations!"[96]

But he allows such "temptations" for his friends, who become rich at the expense of the faithful.

"What do hypocrites do? They disguise themselves, they disguise themselves as good."[97]

He knows that he has a great hypocrite as Coordinator of the Council of Cardinal Advisers and does not care.

---

[94] "Papa: Como Don Milani, asistamos . . ." *op. cit.*

[95] "Pope Francis wants Church to be poor, and for the poor," *Reuters,* March 16, 2013, at https://www.reuters.com/article/us-pope-poor/pope-francis-wants-church-to-be-poor-and-for-the-poor-idUSBRE92F05P20130316.

[96] General Audience, Paul VI Audience Hall, Aug. 8, 2018, at http://w2.vatican.va/content/francesco/en/audiences/2018/documents/papa-francesco_20180808_udienza-generale.html.

[97] "Francesco: 'No ai cristiani ipocriti truccati da santi,'" *La Stampa,* March 18, 2014, at https://www.lastampa.it/vatican-insider/it/2014/03/18/news/francesco-no-ai-cristiani-ipocriti-truccati-da-santi-1.35778885.

"There is no culture in which theft and the abuse of property are legal; human sensibility, in fact, is very sensitive in regard to the defense of property."[98]

In my complaint regarding Pineda I asked for the restitution of what was stolen, and for more than five years I have been completely ignored.

"In consecrated life and in priestly life, [homosexual] affection doesn't fit. Therefore, the Church recommends that people with a strongly rooted tendency of this kind not be accepted to ministry nor to the consecrated life."[99]

But he welcomes them and encourages them by naming them in important positions.

"I'm pained by the evil that they have done to you (Maradiaga)."[100]

But he is not hurt by the evil that his "right arm" does to others.

It is quite clear to us that in these times and under the mantle of Francis, in order to be able to offend freely, one must be a

[98] Text of General Audience, St. Peter's Square, Nov. 7, 2018, at http://www.vatican.va/content/francesco/en/audiences/2018/document s/papa-francesco_20181107_udienza-generale.html.

[99] Statement made by Pope Francis in book-length interview, *La fuerza de la vocación* (Publicaciones Claretinas, 2018), and quoted in "Papa: 'El ministerio o la vida consagrada no es el lugar (de los homosexuales),'" Religion Digital, Nov. 27, 2018, at https://www.religiondigital.org/libros/Papa-ministerio-consagrada-lugar-homosexuales_0_2071292 900.html.

[100] "S.E. Cardenal Rodríguez Maradiaga: el Papa me dijo 'no te preocupes,'" *Vatican News,* Dec. 26, 2017, at https://www.vaticannews.va/es/iglesia/news/2017-12/s-e--cardenal-rodriguez-maradiaga--el-papa-me-dijo--no-te-preocu.html.

priest. To be a child rapist and not to go to jail, you have to be a priest. In order to have money at one's fingertips from looting universities, one has to be the coordinator of the Council of Cardinal Advisers.

By this I do not mean that there are no good cardinals, good bishops and good priests. We know that there are and this crisis will have to end eventually because the Church would not endure long in these conditions. Indeed, we are living in dangerous times. According to the visions and revelations of Anne Catherine Emmerich: "I saw many good pious bishops; but they were weak and wavering, their cowardice often got the upper hand."[101] It is evident that this is exactly what we are already experiencing. The prophecy is being fulfilled.

I also have the impression that the Church is being run like a commercial enterprise that needs advertising to sell its product, and thus, the pope's phrases are thrown as a hook for Catholic tourists to fill St. Peter's Square every Wednesday, and for those who are not properly informed of what is happening, who believe in that advertising without even imagining what is woven behind those walls.

I was present in that square many times, sometimes as a tourist, other times next to my husband representing our country in official ceremonies. Those were the days of the pontificates of John Paul II and Benedict XVI. I also saw the white smoke coming out when Bergoglio was elected and I was at the ceremony of his investiture. I admired him very much for his simplicity, and we were received by him in private audience when we said goodbye as ambassadors at the end of our office in July 2013. We never imagined that, a short time later, I would be deceived and even betrayed by this pope.

---

[101] *The Life and Revelations of Anne Catherine Emmerich: Book 2* (TAN Books, 2014), revelation of July, 1820.

Things never seen

Never in the recent history of the Church were tomatoes thrown at a pope, with churches burned, and people shouting at him "defender of pedophiles." This is what happened in Chile. It is also a rare thing for a prestigious theologian of the highest credibility, such as Fr. Thomas Weinandy, to denounce a pope for his wrongdoing.

It had never been seen that synod participants urged "accepting and valuing [homosexual] sexual orientation," as did the leadership of the 2014 Synod of Bishops in its interim report.[102] Never before had a pope prohibited an Episcopal Conference from implementing reforms for the investigation of sexual abuse, as Francis did to the bishops of the United States.

Never before had a high prelate of the Church asked for the resignation of a pope. This is what the ex-nuncio Viganò did in his impressive document that the pope could not deny. What did Maradiaga say when the Viganò report came out? That he has sinned against the Holy Spirit by asking the pope to resign! As a result, several articles were published that ridiculed Maradiaga for such a statement.

Cardinal Raymond L. Burke, one of the most respected cardinals in the Vatican, said: "It is diabolical to try to adapt the Church to the culture of the world." Now we are seeing the terrible consequences and contradictions of the pope and his self-accusing silence in the face of denunciations like those of Viganò.

---

[102] The English text of the interim report (the "relatio post disceptationem") has been removed from the Vatican website. However the Italian version still remains, which can be found at http://press.vatican.va/content/salastampa/it/bollettino/pubblico/2014/10/13/0751/03037.html.

Every day the news headlines about the pope and his papacy are more surprising:

"Theologians accuse pope of heresy" (Catholic News Agency)

"Vatican scrambles after pope appears to deny existence of hell" (The Guardian)

"Senior liturgist defends attacks on Rome 'idolatry'" (The Tablet)

"Pope Francis says Church should apologise to gay people" (BBC News)

"Pope Francis tells gay man: 'God made you like that and loves you like that'" (CNN)

"Top Theologian Says Francis Presides over 'Internal Papal Schism'" (Breitbart)

"The German Church is in rebellion against Catholic doctrine on homosexuality" (InfoVaticana)

This is to cite a few of the hundreds of articles that document the actions of Pope Francis and his allies defying thousands of years of Catholic doctrine and tradition. Religions cannot change their core doctrines. They cannot distort their values just because times change. The word of God is for eternity. There is only one morality; it cannot be changed because it would cease to be moral.

What used to be abnormal and perverse, they now see as normal. Now immorality is being promoted from the Vatican and the world is falling apart. We appear to be approaching the era of the "great tribulation" mentioned in the Book of Revelation.

This is what the prophecies popularly attributed to Therese Neumann tell us for this epoch so decisive for humanity: "There will come a time when man and the earth will be dirty and corrupt to such an extent that there will be no solution other than the general cleansing of a deluge. But this time it will be a flood of fire." Similar statements are found in the New Testament.[103]

Will the Francis papacy go down in history as a real disaster?

There are too many dark spots. An Argentine friend once asked me if I trusted Pope Francis and I said yes. She thoughtfully told me: "He protected sexual abusers in Argentina. Being Argentine, he hasn't come to Argentina on a visit because it doesn't suit him. In fact, the pope alone in his first four years of pontificate visited 29 countries. He has visited many countries in South America, including those bordering Argentina: Brazil, Chile, Paraguay, Uruguay, Bolivia, Colombia, Ecuador and Panama, but he does not reach his native country." Now I have many reasons not to trust him.

In recent years he has acted weakly against abusers in Chile and it is evident that he did so only because of strong protests and pressure from the media during his trip there. Otherwise, everything would have remained exactly the same because he had done absolutely nothing before that trip. The same thing happened with McCarrick; he wanted to resolve the issue before the episcopal meeting dedicated to clerical pederasty began, while in the past he ignored the sanctions imposed on him by Pope Benedict and sent him on missions around the world.

The same has happened with Bishop Pineda. His resignation must have been forced and they did it surely to release a little pressure on the boiling teapot about to explode. If the media hadn't reported on it, everything would still be the same. But

---

[103] See, for example, 2 Pet. 3:10; 2 Thess. 1:7-8.

Pineda should be in jail, like any other prisoner, paying for his crimes.

In 1962, Pope John XXIII repeated the Catholic Church's long-standing policy of prohibiting people with homosexual tendencies from entering the priesthood, in a secret instruction to bishops called "The Crime of Solicitation." In 2005 Pope Benedict reaffirmed this policy, and even Pope Francis has reaffirmed it since then. However, this policy has been ignored for decades, and many seminaries, like ours in Tegucigalpa, have received many homosexuals as candidates to the priesthood. Now the Catholic faithful are protesting because some of these individuals are sexual abusers and pedophiles who abuse children, and because there are bishops who protect them and there is a pope who covers them up. This chain of cover-ups is undermining the Church considerably. At least I, as a Catholic, do not accept under any circumstances that a priest should consecrate the body and blood of Christ with dirty hands and perverted mind.

Confronted with Viganò's report, the pope refused to respond, and then appeared to defend himself by recommending "silence" for "people who only seek scandal, who seek only division, who seek only destruction," effectively accusing Archbishop Viganò of the same.[104] This is a tremendous contradiction because in the document *Gaudete et exsultate* in which the pope invites us to holiness, he has said: "It is not healthy to love silence while fleeing interaction with others."[105]

Francis is loved by a large percentage of Catholics who see only his friendly and sympathetic side, but who ignore more important and complex issues. There are people like the New

[104] See, "Pope at Mass: 'the truth is humble, the truth is silent'," Vatican News, Sept. 3, 2018, at https://www.vaticannews.va/en/pope-francis/ mass-casa-santa-marta/2018-09/pope-mass-santa-marta-silence-truth- humble-silent.html.

[105] *Gaudete et Exultate*, par. 26, at http://www.vatican.va/content/ francesco/en/apost_exhortations/documents/papa-francesco_ esortazione-ap_20180319_gaudete-et-exsultate.html.

York Times columnist Ross Douthat who already think that his pontificate could be a real disaster, and the theologian Thomas Weinandy has said, "For me, what is presently most troubling is the vague, uncertain and often seemingly nonchalant ecclesial response to the evil, not only to the grievous sexual misconduct among the clergy and bishops, but also to the scandalous undermining of the doctrinal and moral teaching of Scripture and the Church's magisterial tradition."[106]

Monsignor Weinandy, a Capuchin and one of the world's foremost theologians, was forced out of his position as a consultant to the US Conference of Catholic Bishops for sending a public letter to Francis in July of 2017 lamenting the "chronic confusion" in matters of doctrine that reigns in his pontificate and holding the pope accountable.[107] Instead of thanking him for opening his eyes, Francis allowed the American bishops to remove Weinandy.

The famous theologian has written again, this time to affirm that the situation has only worsened. "The Body of Christ presently suffers more than it did then – and I fear the suffering will become even more intense," he warned in October of 2018, bemoaning a world indifferent to evil, not only to gravely sinful sexual conduct in the clergy and episcopate, but also to the scandalous deterioration of the doctrinal and moral teaching of the Scriptures and of the Church's magisterial tradition.[108]

What will happen to Pope Francis, who punishes those who speak in favor of God's principles and favors those who act and speak in favor of Satan? One gets the impression that the devil is gradually taking over the institutions of the Church. That is why Archbishop Viganò tells us that we must take it out of the

---

[106] See, "The Letter: One Year Later," The Catholic Thing, Oct. 31, 2018, at https://www.thecatholicthing.org/2018/10/31/the-letter-one-year-later/.

[107] See "Full Text of Father Weinandy's Letter to Pope Francis," National Catholic Register, Nov. 1, 2017, at https://www.ncregister com/blog/edward-pentin/full-text-of-father-weinandys-letter-to-pope-francis.

[108] *Op. cit.*

stinking swamp it is in. It would be governed by God's principles if the pope put his sayings into practice. His sayings would have substance if they were not carried away by the wind like dry leaves.

How fantastic it would be if the pope's behavior were consistent with so many of his beautiful statements, but they serve only for propaganda, to promote his image with the press and public. The Church would be well governed if the teachings of our Lord Jesus Christ were followed, putting into practice the legacy He left us. The Church would be well governed if the pope had chosen the best elements within it to work on important matters, such as the famous Council of Cardinal Advisers which has had some very questionable members, such as Rodríguez Maradiaga, who is still its coordinator, and Francisco Javier Errázuriz Ossa, who was removed in 2018 following credible accusations of covering up the sexual abuse committed by Fr. Fernando Karadima in Chile.

The Church would be well governed if the pope had listened to Monsignor Thomas Weinandy, and had reprimanded Godfried Danneels, but he did quite the opposite. In a letter by Archbishop Viganò to Cardinal Ouellet asking him to reveal the documents of the McCarrick case, he says: "I told [Pope Francis] that McCarrick had sexually corrupted generations of priests and seminarians, and had been ordered by Pope Benedict to confine himself to a life of prayer and penance. Instead, McCarrick continued to enjoy the special regard of Pope Francis and was given new responsibilities and missions by him. McCarrick was part of a network of bishops promoting homosexuality who, exploiting their favor with Pope Francis, manipulated episcopal appointments so as to protect themselves from justice and to strengthen the homosexual network in the hierarchy and in the Church at large. Pope Francis himself has either colluded in this corruption, or, knowing what he does, is gravely negligent in failing to oppose it and uproot it."

The pope is determined to support and cover up Maradiaga knowing of his corruption and all he is accused of, and that he himself has verified through the investigation made by his friend Pedro Casaretto. However, the limit has been the surprising appointment of Bishop Edgar Peña Parra in a position as important as "Substitute" in the Secretariat of State is the third in order of hierarchy. Viganò in his document says that he had very bad references, and also that documents have been published providing evidence of immoral behavior on his part.

Faced with harsh criticism of Peña Parra, Vatican News published a statement by the leadership of the Venezuelan Episcopal Conference declaring that the accusations are "calumnies" by people who "are seeking to denigrate the institution and undermine the credibility of Pope Francis."[109] It is the same standard, the same pattern that Maradiaga follows, to present themselves as victims in the face of accusations. They have their absurd excuses, their weak defenses and the only thing that they achieve with this is the deterioration of the Church, because nobody believes them anymore.

Everything falls by its weight

As I bring this book to an end, it becomes clear to me that things will continue to fall because of their weight. More and more scandals will be exposed because time is like the sea: the sea brings everything back to shore, from bottles to corpses.

The Catholic University of Honduras is currently undergoing a revolution. The medical students are protesting with annoyance and indignation because the rector, Elio Alvarenga, signed an agreement with the Ministry of Health where they have eliminated the salary of the students who must do a one-year internship before graduating. All medical students, including those at the National University, have received for many decades that salary that, although minimal, helps them to survive.

---

[109] See, "Venezuela: Obispos respaldan a Mons. Edgar Peña Parra tras acusaciones "calumniosas"", Vatican News, Aug. 23, 2019, at https://www.vaticannews.va/es/iglesia/news/2019-08/venezuela-obispos-respaldan-mons-edgar-pena-parra-tras-calumnias.html.

According to a source close to the matter who spoke to me privately after the cardinal was denounced for corruption, the cardinal has asked that the check of one million lempiras (USD 40,000) that he receives monthly from the university no longer be made out in his name but in the name of the diocese, because "people were going around talking about it." It was of no use to the cardinal because the students are not fools and they understand what is going on, that that million could be used to pay their meager salary as medical interns, a salary that has been withheld for years. However, the cardinal has never given an account of this or any other money he has received from the university.

A public letter to Pope Francis

Since time was passing and nothing positive was happening, I decided to send a public letter to Pope Francis. I also gave a copy to the nuncio in Honduras. However, they don't care if it is a private letter or a public letter; either way, they don't answer. They don't care about anything. What they care about is deceiving people with nice phrases and covering up those who engage in cover-ups.

November 7, 2018

Most Reverend Holiness:

I am happy to write to you again to state that I continue praying to God for your pontificate, as you have asked of your noble People of God.

Following the death of my beloved spouse Alejandro Valladares, I have felt in my own person the experiences of that widow of the Holy Gospels, whom our Lord Jesus Christ always understands and exalts, because of her fragile and vulnerable condition in a world that is increasingly more unjust and forgetful of God.

In the same way, I presented myself to you when I had the opportunity on November 21, 2017. I sought you out as the successor of Peter the Apostle and not as the unjust judge of the Gospel of St. Luke (Luke 18:1-8). Afflicted by the immense pain that I have suffered for several years after learning of the financial scam of which my family and I were victims, a scam in which your "friend and right hand" Óscar Rodríguez Maradiaga is directly involved. I must confess to you, Your Holiness, that I returned from that meeting full of hope and joy because of the expectations I felt after dialoguing with you, because I had placed my problem in the hands of the shepherd who feeds the sheep.

Your Holiness, I have believed and trusted you, especially because of the words you spoke to me personally on that 21st of November 2017. "I am aware of your case, I have read your letters and I have already ordered the Secretary of State to resolve your problem. Count on all my goodwill."

At that moment you seemed like a loving Father and I thanked you very much, which you know. However, it saddens me to see that exactly one year has passed, and although I don't like to think this way, I cannot help but see the image of the unjust judge in you, and what I really see is that although we widows are protected by our Lord Jesus Christ in the Holy Scriptures, the one you protect is your "right arm," Cardinal Maradiaga.

Tell me: am I wrong? Tell me: am I personifying that "annoying" widow and am disturbing you, Your Holiness? Tell me: should I insist until you get tired of me and give me justice with regard to Maradiaga? Or is it clear that in my case I am that widow of whom Jesus already speaks in the same gospel of St. Luke, who in any case will soon receive, not the justice of man, but the justice of God, for which I have blind faith? For, in front of everyone, it has been proved with evidence that Maradiaga has covered up for sexual abuse, has been accused of financial dishonesty and other very unpleasant things that I prefer not to mention.

I ask God's spirit to console me and give me the discernment to accept the inexplicable decision you made, at the height of the media scandals provoked by Maradiaga, to reconfirm him in his office after his 75th birthday when he was ready for his retirement as Bishop of Tegucigalpa.

Today, the reason for my letter, Pope Francis, is to consult you with all the respect for your investiture, because you defend and find a cardinal of the Catholic Church who is a disgrace to his country and his noble people, capable of going against all morality and against all Christian principles, accused also by the former nuncio Viganò in his testimony, testimony that regretfully we all know that no one has been able to deny.

You know, Pope Francis, that in the proofs published in various international media against your "right-hand man" Maradiaga, it is clear that for years he has received, from the Catholic University of Honduras, one million lempiras (L. 1,000,000.00) per month plus an extra "bonus" on his birthday for one and a half million lempiras (L. 1,500,000.00) for his personal use and of which he has not given an account to anyone? Many of us wonder why you cover up for him when on the other hand you have said that you "dream of a poor Church for the poor"? Just to give you an example of the damage caused by the removal of this money: today there are thousands of medical students from that university and thousands of poor people who have been deceived as they wait for the construction of two hospitals for their social service and health care internships.

It is not fair, just as it is not fair that a widow should have been deprived of the only resources she had, because she was badly influenced by an ambitious cardinal like Maradiaga (of that you have the proof).

Finally, Your Holiness, regarding your sincerity in telling me to count on all your good will: I am still waiting and insisting, and a year has passed in which you could have demonstrated it, because you are the pope, and as pope you would not have to permit a bad cardinal like Maradiaga to place his will over yours, because if so, it is not the spirit of good that is dominant, but the spirit of evil.

I want to leave a margin of doubt, a margin of hope, hope that we have a true Vicar of Jesus in the world who is capable of placing things in order and doing justice to the widow protected by Christ.

Faithful in Jesus Christ,
Martha Alegría R de Valladares

CHAPTER VII

I CANNOT REMAIN SILENT

I raise my voice

Most holy and dear sweet father in Christ sweet Jesus: I your unworthy daughter Catherine, servant and slave of the servants of Jesus Christ, write to you in his precious Blood. . . . Do you uproot in the garden of Holy Church the malodorous flowers, full of impurity and avarice, swollen with pride: that is, the bad priests and rulers who poison and rot that garden. Ah me, you our Governor, do you use your power to pluck out those flowers! Throw them away, that they may have no rule! Insist that they study to rule themselves in holy and good life. Plant in this garden fragrant flowers, priests and rulers who are true servants of Jesus Christ, and care for nothing but the honor of God and the salvation of souls, and the fathers of the poor.

St. Catherine of Sienna to Pope Gregory XI

I don't intend to hurt anyone with this book. In this case, those who have suffered harm have been harmed by their own actions. By revealing the facts, what I am trying to do is to help stop the enormous damage that our Holy Mother Church is suffering. I intend to open the eyes of Catholics so that they do not take part in that complicity that is directly offending God. I am joining others who are crying out, who are seeking to rescue our Church from the filth in which it is submerged. I raise my voice in an enormous cry to say: Enough! No one mocks God!

If Catherine of Siena, being a saint, seven centuries ago wrote a letter to the pope launching this same cry, why shouldn't I do it, even if I am not a saint? I can do it because I profess that same love for Christ who is being crucified again every day in his own house. It seems that we are approaching the time of "The Great Tribulation" because the Church's internal enemies are attempting to convert the Church into the "Whore" spoken of in Revelation chapter 17.

It's not just a few people; it's a whole people that reproaches Cardinal Rodríguez Maradiaga, including Catholics. With the many millions of lempiras that the Catholic University of Honduras receives, it could be the best in Central America and could have built the two hospitals it should have built many years ago, but the millions are diverted for dark purposes while the students protest in the streets, demanding their rights instead of studying in the laboratories while their parents get into debt. What an example of honesty! What an example of Christianity!

In the midst of the storm I praise God

As I had explained before, from the moment I realized that we had lost everything, I was certain that we were going to get it back and my daughter was amazed at my calm reaction. By the way, recently she told me: "Mother, I was afraid to tell you because I thought you were going to run out and throw yourself in front of a train."

Another friend said to me: "I am impressed by your strength because I met a man who lost everything and, faced with his helplessness, committed suicide." I know that the difference lies in having faith, or not having faith. That's just what makes the difference. Faith is what has kept me serene, making my life normal, enjoying it filled with hope, and believing in God's promises.

Another person related to me a case of a friend who was robbed by two associates of all the millions invested in a project; seeking to comfort him, he listed the things he had left and the friend replied: "But they were my friends!" The obviously destroyed and traumatized man cried and cried until he committed suicide. He could not bear the two tragedies together. I have been bearing them for four years.

I do not want to deny that I have had very difficult moments. I have wept for the indignation of seeing myself outraged by the powerful, by someone stronger who protects himself with the shield of lies and falsehood and silence. Many believe the lies just as I believed them, but my story is true. And not just mine, but also that of many others who have testified about the corruption in the Church.

I owe myself to God and to God alone. I understand that there must be many people who want to judge me or who have judged me, who may think I am a slanderer, but it is time that resolves everything. An example of this is the case I recounted above of Father José de Jesús Mora, who proclaimed the truth, but was threatened, intimidated and humiliated so much that his disappointment was so great that he abandoned the priesthood. If the cardinal thought he had fixed the problem in this way, he was totally mistaken because it remained latent. He might have fixed it if he had sent Erick Cravioto back to Mexico and put his house in order.

I am sure that José de Jesús Mora is now very satisfied because what he denounced many years ago is now being denounced by Catholic newspapers throughout the world. In other words, time has proved him right. That's how simple divine justice works.

One very important thing for me is to have a clear conscience, not to feel guilty, because otherwise I would be destroying myself by being unable to sleep, and for me it is extremely important to go to bed in peace to have a happy dream. If it were not so, I would surely be in the hands of psychologists or psychiatrists, because it was no small thing: I lost my husband, who died a very painful death, when I least expected it. A short time later I lost all the family savings and then I was terribly betrayed, not once, not twice, but many times. But the worst thing is that I have not been betrayed by ordinary people but by those who wear a crucifix on their chest and a skullcap on their head.

I have lived through a lot, I know. I would never have thought that I could withstand so many blows from human beings, which have struck my life like merciless hurricanes driven by dark forces. But they have not been able to destroy either my faith or my hope. They have not been able to tear from my soul the love of Christ because it is on Him that all my strength depends.

In the midst of this storm, I praise the good God. In the midst of this storm, I smile at life, because my life . . . remains always beautiful! Beautiful, because I have nothing to hide. Beautiful, because I sleep peacefully. Because I am free. Because God sends me his grace. Beautiful, because God loves me and I feel his evident love. Beautiful, because I believe in his promises. Isaiah 41:17 states, "I will open rivers in the high bills, and fountains in the midst of the plains: I will turn the desert into pools of waters, and the impassable land into streams of waters." God will not forsake me. I take that for granted. Therefore my life cannot be invaded by despair or destroyed by pain.

The psychological problems I could suffer could be enormous, however, I have remained serene; no one ever noticed that I was going through something so terrible. More than one person has said to me, "Why haven't you had a heart attack?" It is God who has sustained me. It is God who has stood by my side, it is God who has guided me, who continues to guide me and it is he in whom I have trusted. "God alone is enough."

I follow the path that God is tracing for me. I remember that when the cardinal refused to meet me in Rome, I thought: "Well, this means that God wants me to unmask this false prophet. Well, so it will be." The interview came out.

I have been contacted by people that I didn't even know existed. They have appeared as angels who have come down from heaven to help me and support me in my struggle. This can only come from God.

A few days ago I told my youngest daughter that we had to have a little more patience, and remember that "God writes straight with crooked lines," and she, with her great sense of humor, answered me: "Well, let's buy a notebook for God with straight lines."

I am bringing this rottenness to light head-on. I know that there are so many people, so many people, including priests, who are indignant at the falsehood of the cardinal and his assistant. They say it, they share it, but they do almost nothing. They do nothing out of the same fear, because for the little they have been able to do, they have been punished.

A friend said to me: "Are you aware that you are fighting a Mafia?" Yes! But this is the task God has for me.

Mercy and hope

I have always considered my life wonderful because God has always been generous to me. Having gone through this great suffering, I always consider it marvelous because I feel that he has chosen me his instrument to bring to light what he has wished me to bring to light, although I can only refer to what has happened to me and to my surroundings.

I still consider it marvelous because in the midst of so much injustice I have not been invaded by hatred, rancor or bitterness. There are moments when I feel totally helpless, crushed by that lacerating power capable of destroying anyone, and my pain becomes more acute . . . but suddenly, God enables me to receive his message and fills me with a new strength and new hope.

How can I not believe in the power and mercy of God? He is omnipotent. He is the one who has the true power over the universe, over the earth and over men. Pineda, Maradiaga and

Francisco are simple mortals whom one day God will ask for an account of their actions. My life is wonderful because God has me in a crucible testing my faith and I am sure of my loyalty. There are times when I have felt like Job, where the devil has fought to make me feel desperate and to deny the good God, but he has not succeeded and will not succeed.

God is my hope, God is my refuge, my light and my guide. Without him I would be invaded by madness. It is he who sustains me, keeps me lucid, firm and courageous fighting like a David against a Goliath. There is no worse indignation than feeling like an insect under a steel boot, but under that steel boot I have been able to kick, I have been able to shout the truth to the world . . . and they have listened to me.

I consider my life wonderful because my pain has awakened hearts and there have been reactions that have relieved me as a refreshing balm. I consider my life wonderful because I have the opportunity to suffer and feel embraced by the Jesus who suffers on his cross. I consider my life wonderful because God is wonderful and I feel him with me. I feel him by my side, and if God is with me, who can stand against me?

I couldn't stay quiet

It is truly sad to have had to write this story because it is a horrible story, one that is horrible above all for Holy Mother Church. But writing it I know that I have made a small contribution to the effort to clean it up.

I am convinced that those who are dirty cannot hide behind doors or under carpets. The house must always be clean, full of pure and perfumed air – especially the house of God.

As a victim of the system that is currently governing the Church, it is impossible to keep my mouth shut. I know that to keep all this quiet for the rest of my life would be an impossible burden to bear, and as several people have told me, this story has to be known because it would not be fair, after so much wrong has been done in secret, to bury things as if nothing had happened. Moreover, the cardinal ended up proving that he was never our friend. While we thought he was, we were always loyal, faithful and grateful to him, but now that we know him to be the most sadistic enemy, I don't have to be silent. No gentlemen, to be silent would make me your accomplice.

I repeat Luke 12, 1-3: "Beware ye of the leaven of the Pharisees, which is hypocrisy. For there is nothing covered, that shall not be revealed: nor hidden, that shall not be known.
For whatsoever things you have spoken in darkness, shall be published in the light: and that which you have spoken in the ear in the chambers, shall be preached on the housetops."

Personally, I am convinced that we should not leave everything in God's hands, nor should we commit so many sins of omission. I think we should also put into practice those thoughts popularly attributed to wise people like Edmund Burke, Albert Einstein and Mahatma Gandhi:

"For evil to triumph, it is enough that good men do nothing."

"The world is in danger not because of evil people but because of those who allow evil."

"The most atrocious of the bad things of bad people is the silence of good people."

"The inner voice tells me not to fear this world, but to go forward carrying in me nothing but the fear of God."

In writing this story I feel that I have honored these wise sayings. I am certain that God placed me at this crossroads to play a role, and I have played the role that he chose for me. I am grateful for the support of so many priests who said to me: Keep it up!

Without a doubt, one of the things that drove me to continue writing this book were these verses from the Holy Scriptures that providentially came to me at the right moment: "Be strengthened in the Lord and in the might of his power. Put you on the armor of God, that you may be able to stand against the deceits of the devil" (Eph. 6: 10-11) and, "Have no fellowship with the unfruitful works of darkness: but rather reprove them. For the things that are done by them in secret, it is a shame even to speak of. But all things that are reproved are made manifest by the light: for all that is made manifest is light" (Eph. 5: 11-13). This I never tire of repeating because this is my flag and this will be my victory!

In the storm: a poem

No quiero ser ave buscando refugio atrapada en la recia tormenta ni temerosa quiero agacharme para dejarla pasar.

I do not wish to be a bird seeking refuge while trapped in a harsh storm, crouching in fear to let it pass.

No quiero ser cruelmente fulminada por un rayo implacable ni envuelta por un remolino de viento salvaje.

I do not wish to be cruelly struck down by implacable lightning nor enveloped by a wild wind.

No quiero dejarme abatir ni me puedo quebrantar. Decidí, como el águila por encima de la tormenta . . . volar.

I do not wish to let myself be toppled, nor broken. I decided, like the eagle above the storm . . . to fly.

Martha Alegría, January 2018

APPENDIX

Corruption at Catholic University led to fall of Cardinal Rodrguez[110]

Confidencial Honduras

July 28, 2016

TEGUCIGALPA, HONDURAS

A colossal network of asset laundering, administrative mis-management, illicit enrichment, homosexuality and persecution of dissidents and waste of multimillion-dollar resources is bringing to light a great network of corruption at the Catholic University of Honduras (UNICAH).

Extensive documents in the possession of Radio Globo and Confidencial Honduras expose this network of corruption headed by Cardinal Óscar Andres Rodríguez and Rector Elio David Alvarenga Amador, who, in alliance with the head of the Catholic Church in the capital, Juan Jose Pineda, have orchestrated a plot of corruption, intrigue and other elements that exhibit the moral baseness of those who preside over the Catholic Church.

---

[110] Published at https://confidencialhn.com/corrupcion-en-universidad-catolica-orillo-caida-de-cardenal-rodriguez/.

An extensive document to which both media have had access shows how Rodríguez orchestrated a very sophisticated network of money transfers that filled his pocket, and in 13 years appropriated some 130 million lempiras.

In fact, in order to fully comply with the plans of control, domination and submission, the cardinal and the rector of the university, in collusion with [Auxiliary Bishop] Pineda, proceeded to carry out large-scale purges – in other words, they sent away people who could be detrimental to the interests of this trio, sending them abroad to complete their masters and doctorates. Others, such as the good priest Ovidio Rodríguez, were ostracized; today he is the priest of an infrequently-visited chapel.

With the arrival of Pineda in 2005 (to the archbishop's residence) a large scale purge was carried out. Ovidio Rodríguez was left in a small parish at the Catholic University. Juan José Pineda became a divisive force in the archdiocese and asked for the cardinal's support to the detriment of all of the priests, and persecuted the dissidents: some were sent to distant parishes, others exiled to study and others were ostracized.

The document, prepared by priests and laity committed to restoring decency in the church and UNICAH, uses several phrases of Pope Francis who has condemned corruption in all its forms, and condemn the position taken by the cardinal and his assistants, who have abandoned moral and Christian values for the culture of power-worship.

The document explains how the cardinal and Juan José Pineda, a dark character recognized for his marked homosexuality despite condemning such practices in the pulpit, had access to resources that were so unlimited that Pineda himself has asked to build a residence on the campus of UNICAH, a residence without specific functions.

"His relationship with the clergy has been disrespectful, and his homosexuality is well known. As pastor of the church he has no known achievements, his homosexuality is widely known, and there are attacks on other people, and he has an agreement with the rector, and the cardinal receives funds from the rectory for personal expenses," states the research document, which Confidencial HN was able to view.

RELIGIOUS RACISM. According to the document, the National Congress decorated the cardinal for his "collaborationism" with regard to the the dictatorial government of Roberto Micheletti; the award was presented in the UNICAH facilities and not in the Parliament where these awards are usually given.

The report explains that the 137 members of the archdiocese of Tegucigalpa chose not to go to the event, enraging Pineda, who immediately sent to fill the convention hall with students who were forced to attend the event, under penalty of being punished.

Likewise, by awarding the cardinal at the University, he gave the bishop carte blanche so that he could exercise strict entrance controls. It was he who decided whether or not the guests could be present at the event.

Pineda is said to have taken some 88 million lempiras.

OBSCURE RELATIONSHIPS. The control of the university by the cardinal and entourage allowed the perpetuation of nepotism or "family" as the authors of the report say.

The rector's relatives have participated in the distribution of cushy jobs and are the main actors in the whole plot. He is accompanied by his cousin Misael Arguijo Alvarenga and his wife Lourdes Fortín and other employees of his choice.

It is worth mentioning that Arguijo has a bad reputation for being a sexual harasser, leading to two divorces, one in Santa Rosa de Copán and the other in SPS; two subordinates were involved in these sinful plots.

The authors point to Arguijo as one who engages in cover-ups and, at present, is the head of automation, with another cousin. He is responsible for the disastrous computer system and is responsible for the Catholic Church's media systems, including Suyapa Tv, Radio Católica and the weekly Fides.

The report states that a Channel 48 vehicle was assigned to his wife, who is known in university circles as "the first academic lady." The university pastorate is directed by a dentist who assumed the deanship full time and did not leave his position at the National Autonomous University of Honduras (UNAH).

The teacher arrived at his office at UNAH, leaving a wallet to pretend he was at work, but escaped to fulfill his role at the Catholic University. "This is the best example of the fraud," says the document, adding that he managed to move on to pastoral work.

The rector intended to elevate UNICAH to a Pontifical Catholic University, while a cult of personality was created around him, going to the extreme of imposing mystical religious visions.

The researchers had access to the testimony of members of the faithful who teach at the University, students and people committed to the cause, who asked for anonymity to avoid persecution from the authorities of the education center.

THE CARDINAL'S EXPENSES. The person responsible for running the university has maintained a double accounting system: he tells the members of the center of studies that there is no money and the little that is perceived is distributed in the Honduran churches. But on the other books, of which the cardinal is aware, there are some one billion lempiras that they have received from the students and other contributions.

So far, an audit report revealing the use of the funds by Catholic University authorities has not been submitted.

In the double accounting report, it is revealed that the rector is transferring one million lempiras per month to Maradiaga and in December he received around 2.5 million lempiras, making a total of 13 million.

In the 13 years of transfers, there is a count of 130 million lempiras received by the cardinal for personal expenses and these funds are used without effective accountability. Moreover, it is pointed out that the money is directed to personal expenses.

On the other hand, the other members of the university faculty only receive 300,000 lempiras for basic expenses. The funds assigned to the bishops are to help the dioceses, and the justification is that UNICAH has no profits and the rest is used to build facilities.

According to estimates, teachers have lost 115 million lempiras in labor benefits.

FALLEN INTO DISGRACE. The greed of the university leadership went so far as to promote layoffs and cuts in labor rights for the staff working at the school.

"The last one to fall was Ricardo Donohue; Virginia de Avilés, Gustavo Izaguirre, Martha Abarca, Virgilio Solis, Vilma Espinal, Mario Meraz, Raúl Díaz Velásquez, Mercedes Grisaleñan, Karen Heinze, Guadalupe Ramos, Mirna Rosales, Sandra Velásquez and others were also fired," the investigation reveals.

The ambitions of Rector Elio Alvarenga led to the misfortune of Cardinal Rodríguez, also lost the opportunity of his life to assume a position in the Vatican.

The cardinal, faced with this mega-scandal, was replaced by four bishops who will direct the destinies of the Catholic Church. In addition, the cardinal now has less than a year to retire, so his retirement will be a very dark one, as will be the allegations of corruption that have been revealed by a group of priests and lay people aspiring to bring about a reform of UNICAH.

Bishops Angel Garachana Perez, Hector Garcia. Hector Camilleri and Guido Charbonell will be responsible for the rescue of the millenary church. Likewise, the cardinal and his trusted servants will no longer be able to choose at will the superior, intermediate and inferior commanders of the Catholic Church.

They say that in an assembly of the Episcopal Conference of Honduras, Bishop Garachana confronted the cardinal, saying: "Have you taken money from the university? I remind you that the university is a good of the church." Silence was the answer and, for that reason, he was removed from the Episcopal Conference.

The new leadership has committed itself to take the church to the poorest and to be more loyal to the parishioners, who were abandoned by the Catholic hierarch who opted for the tinsel and neon that power offers.

For now it is not known if the ex-papabile will be accountable for 130 million lempiras.

In December 2015, the cardinal canceled a dinner for the Catholic clergy as well as their bonus of 25,000 lempiras. Those affected asked the religious leader about it and he reacted with annoyance: "It's because you denounced me to the apostolic nuncio."

THREE ROSES FOR PINEDA. Meanwhile, Pineda saw his dreams of being the visible head of the Catholic Church in Danlí frustrated. He was ordered to return to Tegucigalpa and has asked to be installed on the Tres Rosas campus in the village of Valle de Angeles.

It is not known what the future of the Catholic bishop will be.

ABOUT THE AUTHOR

Martha Alegría Reichmann de Valladares is the widow of the former ambassador to the Holy See for Honduras and Dean of the Vatican Diplomatic Corps, Alejandro Emilio Valladares Lanza. She was born in Honduras in 1946, and was trained in Canada as a bilingual secretary. She has lived in Rome since 1991. Her oil paintings have been displayed in more than 50 exhibitions both individually and collectively in various countries. In addition to *Sacred Betrayals*, she has written three books of spiritual poetry and narrative, one of which, "Yo te encontré," ("I found you") was published by the Vatican in 2013. Her most recent book, published in Honduras, is *Cartas al Cielo* (Letters to Heaven). She is a member of the Order of the Most Holy Savior of St. Bridget, and has been awarded a medal and honorary degree by the International Academy of Dioscuri.

ABOUT THE TRANSLATOR

Matthew Cullinan Hoffman is an essayist and journalist whose articles have appeared in numerous publications worldwide, both secular and Catholic, including the *Wall Street Journal*, *London Sunday Times*, *New York Daily News*, LifeSite News, the *National Catholic Register*, *Catholic World Report*, Crisis Magazine, and many others. He is the translator and author of *The Book of Gomorrah and St. Peter Damian's Struggle Against Ecclesiastical Corruption* (Ite ad Thomam, 2015). He holds an M.A. in Philosophy from Holy Apostles College and Seminary, where he is certified for academic proficiency in five foreign languages.

Made in the USA
Coppell, TX
13 June 2021